Friends
Helping
Friends

A Manual for Peer Counselors

D1310964

by

Carol Painter

Publisher—

Educational Media Corporation®
P.O. Box 21311
Minneapolis, MN 55421-0311

(612) 781-0088

Production editor—

Don L. Sorenson

Graphic design—

Earl Sorenson

To Cherise, my friend of friends
To Tim and Lisa, who create a world of love
and
To all the peer counselors I have known and loved

Table of Contents

A Letter to Peer Counselors

Dear Peer Counselor:

In opening this book, you have just taken the first step in a journey that may change your life and the lives of others in many special ways. You will have the opportunity to perform a service that cannot be accomplished by anyone else in quite the same way. You have a priceless gift to offer others—the gift of yourself.

As you give of yourself, you will be learning to be a better friend. You will be a friend to people who otherwise would never have known you cared about them. You will be a friend to others who may be different from you in many ways. In all the different people you will meet, the thing they will have in common is their need for a special friend. They need the kind of friend who can help them recognize their strengths. They need someone who can help them see they have a life worth living—even during times when it hurts.

To do this very important and special job requires that you receive some very important and special training. Part of the training will involve an opportunity for you to deal with some of your own painful feelings. To be effective helpers, you have to be able to deal with your own feelings first. Unless you are growing, you cannot help others to grow.

Another important part of the training involves learning the skills of helping. There are several identifiable skills that every effective helper possesses. Some of these skills may be ones you have already developed. This happens because some people are what we call "natural helpers." Yet, a sad thing happens in every training group. The people who have a natural gift for helping sometimes choose to rely on the talent they have, rather than working to develop their full potential. Because they don't work to improve their skills, they don't grow. Because they don't grow, they are not as effective as those who become totally involved in the training experience.

A third important part of the training involves providing information to you on topics such as grief, divorce, chemical dependency, and many others. This will give you the background you need to work effectively with other young people. You also will learn when and how to make referrals to a professional, since some situations call for more expertise than you will possess. As part of this process, you will meet many professionals from your school and community. These people will then be a part of your helping network.

Of all that you will learn this year, though, the greatest will be learning to be a better friend to yourself. This is actually one of the hardest lessons most of us have to learn. However, when we finally learn how to be our own best friend, the world becomes a more positive place. Then we begin to understand that there are no real failures. There are only lessons. These lessons simply become the stepping stones in our journey of personal growth. The most that we can give to ourselves, and to each other, is to become the best that we can be.

In his book, *Illusions*, Richard Bach said, "Argue for your limitations, and sure enough, they're yours." This is what you do every time you say, "I can't." So, from this moment on, rather than saying "I can't" when you encounter a new or difficult situation, say either "I won't" or "I will." Work to stretch yourself and to see yourself as being capable of doing—or learning to do—anything that you really want to do. You will begin to glimpse new possibilities in your life. You will begin to see that you can achieve anything that you can dream and are willing to work to bring into reality.

My love and respect,

Carol Painter

Unit I
Helper Development

Chapter 1
Pitfalls on the Path to Helping

In becoming effective helpers, it is important for us to have a clear philosophy of helping and to understand some of the possible "pitfalls." You may or may not agree with what is expressed here. However, what is important is that you decide how *you* feel about each of these issues.

Being Your Own Best Friend

Being helpers requires that we maintain a balance in our own lives so that we have extra energy and love to give to others. This can only happen if we are able to give ourselves positive acknowledgement and support, rather than constant critical judgment of all we do. The "pitfall" for most of us is that we are afraid that if we see ourselves as good people, then we will stop being good people! The belief seems to be that the only way we can remain good people is to see ourselves as bad people!

However, consider for a moment what relationships would be like based upon this belief system. In these relationships, if we want to see our friends grow and improve, we constantly must remind them of past failures, hurtful words and deeds, and all the times they were inadequate. If someone else tries to remind our friends of their good points and special qualities, we will say, "Yes, maybe so, but usually they just don't live up to my expectations."

It is hard to picture a friendship based on this kind of relationship, isn't it? Why do you suppose this describes the way most of us treat ourselves? What we would never do to someone else is exactly what we do to ourselves, regularly.

Most of us live lives that are out of balance in this way. We can tell someone instantly all that is "wrong" with us. However, when we are asked to describe our strengths, it takes us a great deal longer! It *is* true that we all need to look at the ways we can improve. However, if this is not balanced by acknowledging the things that we do well, we will only succeed in making it feel like a hopeless struggle. We all grow best in an atmosphere of acceptance and love, including the atmosphere we create for ourselves. Personal growth needs to be seen as the exciting challenge that it is, not as a punishment that we inflict on ourselves. What we hope to give to our friends must begin with ourselves.

Selfishness

This is one of the most difficult of all helper issues. The feeling of most beginning helpers is that they must be ready to give people what they need, whenever they need it. When we are feeling strong and things are going well, this is sometimes possible for a short time.

However, most of the time this is just not realistic or even truly helpful! At these times, we need to remember that we cannot give more than we have. If we believe that we must stay in the "role" of helper at all times, we will soon find that we become dangerously overextended. Then we end up withdrawing from the person or the situation abruptly, causing the very pain we were trying to avoid in the first place! The "pitfall" here is in learning when we must say no to a request. If we do not save enough of ourselves for ourselves, we will have nothing left to give others. In other words, selfishness is not always bad, and it is often necessary.

Also, if we help others because we think we "should," but it isn't what we really want to do, people quickly sense it. They come away feeling that they are in our debt and "owe" us. This kind of "helping" can become a hostile act and will create resentment, rather than respect, between people.

It is important to recognize that everything we do is selfish. We do all of the things we do because they make us feel good or because we get something out of doing them. Helping is no exception. We have all chosen to be helpers because we help ourselves every time we help someone else. True helping comes from the heart and can only be given freely and because we truly enjoy the feeling of giving to others.

Responsibility

This is not a word that many young people like to hear very often, probably because they do hear it so often. However, the concept of responsibility is one of the most empowering, and misunderstood, ideas that exists. Most of us think of responsibility as having to do things that we do not want to do. However, responsibility is actually personal power, and this understanding will change our entire approach to life.

When we recognize that we have responsibility in a situation, it follows that we also have control in that situation! By changing our actions, we can change the way others react to us. In taking responsibility, we move away from a "victim" or "blaming" stance. Instead, we take control of our lives and begin to make the changes that we want to see happen.

Many people are afraid of taking responsibility for their relationships, their feelings, and their lives. They are actually more comfortable letting others decide for them, feeling somehow that it is easier. The thinking goes something like this: "If I decide what I want, and I do it, and I don't like the way it turns out, then I will have only myself to blame. So, it is easier to let others decide for me, because at least then I will have them to blame if things don't turn out the way I want." There is actually no harder way to live. Very few of us like decisions that someone else makes for us because it isn't what we would have done! Taking responsibility for ourselves frees us to change our thoughts which changes our actions which changes our reality.

Feelings

One of the most important aspects of helping involves encouraging others to be aware of and honest about their feelings. However, beginning helpers often are afraid that having people focus on their feelings will just make them feel worse, especially when those feelings are strong and painful.

We do no service to people in helping them hide from their feelings. When feelings seem overwhelming or situations seem hopeless, young people in particular are prone to tell each other to just "blow it off." This is intended to be helpful, but it is actually a way of minimizing what a person is feeling and experiencing. The person telling someone to "blow it off" is actually caught in the trap of believing that people are victims of their feelings and have no power.

The reality is that we all *choose* our feelings. You cannot *make* me angry because of something you do. If I feel angry, it is because I choose to feel that way. How else can you explain the fact that some things make some people angry and not others? Our feelings are caused by our thoughts. It is not what happens to us, but what we *think* about what happens to us that determines how we feel.

For example, let's say that when you leave class today to go to your locker, the guy at the locker next to yours takes one look at you and says, "Nerd!" If you *think* that he is right, you are probably going to *feel* depressed. On the other hand, if you *think* that he must be having a pretty bad day to take his anger out on you for no reason, you might *feel* surprised that he is so out of control. You could decide that it is not important and choose to forget all about it.

We can change our feelings by changing our thoughts. By *thinking* differently about anything that happens, we can *feel* differently about it also. This is why it is true to say that there is *always* something that we can do about any situation. We can always choose to feel differently about it.

Accepting Without Question the "Faces" People Wear

We all have the same feelings, fears, and needs. The difference between us is only a matter of degree. For example, we have all felt angry at some time. I may only feel angry occasionally, whereas you may often feel angry. Regardless, anger is an emotion we have both experienced. I may show my anger by withdrawing and being quiet, and you may show your anger by throwing things. If you and I let ourselves be separated by the different ways we have chosen to deal with the same feeling, we will miss the connection between us.

Besides having different ways of dealing with the same feelings, we also have different ways of dealing with the same fears and needs. One of the needs we all have is to be accepted and liked by others. So, one of the fears we have is that we won't be accepted and liked by others. Some people deal with this feeling by becoming extremely shy and introverted. Other people deal with the same feeling by becoming tremendous braggarts. They give others the idea that they are extremely satisfied with themselves. Yet, as is so often true with people, things are just the opposite of the way they seem. If we don't look closely, we will miss the fact that both people have the same fear, but different ways of expressing it.

When we are able to accept others no matter what "face" they wear, it sets up a gracious, as opposed to a vicious, cycle in our lives. The more we are able to accept and understand others, the better we are able to accept and understand ourselves. The more we are able to accept and understand ourselves, the better we are able to accept and understand others.

Seeing "Problems" as Problems

How we see problems determines the quality of our interventions. If we see problems as a terrible load that everyone must carry through life, it affects how we respond to people when they are having problems. We will unconsciously feel pity for them and wonder why they are so unlucky. Unfortunately, when people sense this attitude in those around them, it just confirms what they already thought was true. As a result, their feelings of helplessness and self-pity are reinforced.

However, if we see problems as opportunities for growth, we transmit a completely different attitude. It appears that life is intended to be difficult at times. If it were too easy, we wouldn't grow. If we spent an entire life without challenge, we would end it without having learned all we could.

Of course, no one welcomes problems with open arms and joy! I believe we all enjoy the trouble-free times more than the times when we feel plagued with problems. However, when we truly understand that our problems come to us in order to help us learn a lesson we need, it becomes a completely different experience. Then we will put all of our energy into asking ourselves what it is we need to learn rather than asking ourselves why this had to happen to us!

The ironic part of this is that the better we get at dealing with our problems, the fewer problems we will have. The "pitfall" for the helper is in forgetting that the "bad" times are also the times of growth.

Excellence Without Practice

People who want to be olympic diving champions, for example, would never consider that they could accomplish their dreams without a great deal of practice over the space of many years. Most people also quickly learn that talent alone will not get them there without a great deal of trial and error and dedication to go with it.

If you have ever learned to drive a car with a stick shift, you have a wonderful mental picture of the process we all go through when we learn to do something for the first time. There are the stop and go starts, the grinding gears, and the stalled engine in the middle of a busy intersection to remind us that we are going to need more practice before we can be as smooth and natural as we would like.

However, have you ever noticed that people expect to become an expert in their relationships with only one try? Take for example the young woman who decides to be more assertive in dealing with her boyfriend, but when he snaps at her instead of listening, she decides that assertiveness doesn't really work. Or, what about the young man who decides to confront his father with the derogatory way his father talks to him? However, when he ends up grounded for two months, the young man decides that it is entirely too dangerous to ever tell anyone how he honestly feels.

Our olympic divers undoubtedly had numerous experiences of leaving the diving board sure they were about to deliver a perfect dive and then landing flat on their faces in the water. Somehow, we all seem to accept this condition when we are trying to perfect a physical skill. There is no embarrassment or feeling of failure, but rather a dedication to work all the harder the next day. However, when we are trying to perfect an emotional or interpersonal skill, we often decide after one attempt that we can't do it! If we can't deliver a smooth and perfect result the first time, too often we decide that it is better to stay with what we know, even if it means being miserable.

Advice-Giving

One of the most common misconceptions of good counseling is that it is giving good advice. Counseling is *never* advice-giving! One of the most important things you will learn in your training is how to be of help to others without telling them what they "should" do. You will learn to be a caring and effective listener, offering a different perspective on a situation and facilitating the person's own problem-solving process.

There are many "pitfalls" in giving advice. The greatest of these is if we always solve people's situations for them, they will never learn to do it for themselves. This means each time they have a problem, they are going to need us to solve it for them! A second great problem with advice-giving is we might give advice which has disastrous consequences for a person. An important question which has to be answered by every helper is how responsible are we for the results of our advice-giving? A third problem with giving advice is we hear only one side of an issue when we talk to someone. By giving advice without knowing the whole story, we can actually make a situation worse by reinforcing problem behaviors.

The ironic part about advice-giving is people often ask for it, but they rarely like it. Have you ever had people ask you what they should do, but when you suggested something, they said "Yes, but..." and gave you a lot of reasons why it wouldn't work? We call those "ya-buts." If you are getting a lot of ya-buts from a person, it is a clear signal you are advice-giving, and the person is resisting. Frequently, when people ask for advice, what they are really asking for is our attention and concern, even if they don't quite say so.

There are also times when a person *really* wants to know what we think about a situation. In deciding to give this feedback, however, it is very important how we choose to offer it. The best way I can share *my* perspective on *your* situation is to tell you what I *think* I *might* do *if* I were in *your* situation. This usually stimulates further discussion, which is the most helpful part of the process. In helping, we must never forget each of us has all of our own answers inside.

Needing to Always Make the "Right" Decision

It would be nice if every decision we ever made was the "right" one, meaning that we never later regretted our choice. However, for some people, this need becomes an obsession. They find that their need to make the "right" decision is so great that they become overwhelmed by the process. Rather than getting better at making decisions, any decision becomes almost impossible. Then, rather than risk making the "wrong" decision, they simply float along waiting for other events or people to make their decisions for them.

The only way it would be possible to make only "right" decisions would be to know in advance what will happen. In some cases, we can make fairly accurate predictions as to what will happen if we choose to do a certain thing. However, much of the time we simply cannot know what lies in the future. After doing all possible information gathering, it comes down to a choice on our part. Then we need to make what appears to be the *best* decision and work to *make* it be right! In other words, we need to *make* it work or to use it as a learning process.

If we understand that we will not always do the perfect thing at the right time, we can focus on accepting where we are and then moving closer to where we want to be. Progress becomes a series of short zig zag lines that over time point clearly in the direction we are heading. The "pitfall" lies in believing that the only progress that is acceptable is that of a straight, unbroken line.

Trying

We do not "try" to do things. We either do them, or we do not do them. For example, you cannot "try" to stand. You will either be sitting, or you will be standing. What we think of as "trying to stand" is something we do while we are still sitting!

The word "try" is a good one to take out of your vocabulary. Replace it instead with expressions which indicate whether you will or will not do something. For example, rather than saying, "I'll try to call you tonight," say, "I will make time to call you tonight" or "I will not be calling you tonight."

Notice the shift in focus and control that occurs when we express ourselves in this way. Rather than offering excuses to others, or ourselves, for doing or not doing something, we remind ourselves that ultimately what we do is our choice. Our self-talk, the words we use to communicate with ourselves, carries a great deal of power in determining our choices and needs to be monitored with care.

Be Healthy

Many people now believe most, if not all, diseases are emotional in origin. In other words, we make ourselves sick. As a personal example, years ago I noticed every time I became sick, it was on a Friday night. Then I realized when I didn't feel well during the week, I would continually tell myself I couldn't afford to be sick. When Friday night came, I unconsciously told myself *now* I could afford to be sick! When I recognized what I was doing, I said, "Hold everything! Maybe now I have time to be sick, but I have no desire to be sick!" So, since I had no time during the week and no interest on the week-end, the only solution was to stop being sick altogether.

It has been over ten years since I discovered this way of thinking. In that time, I have had the flu only once. When I show symptoms of something, I say to myself repeatedly, "I don't have time to be sick. I don't want to be sick." I mean it when I say it, and I also ask myself if I need to be doing something to take better care of myself.

People often cause their illnesses by not understanding how their minds work. When they aren't feeling well, they will say repeatedly, "I don't feel well. I'm getting sick." Our bodies are designed for health, but our subconscious minds follow our directions, even to the point of making us sick.

As a helper, it is important for you to develop your own techniques for maintaining physical and emotional health. During your training, you will be exposed to many new ideas and experiences. If you are absent, you will miss opportunities which may not come again. As importantly, others will begin to depend on your "being there." Consistency is an extremely important part of what you do.

The "pitfall" with this topic often comes in the form of disbelief. This is a concept which many people resist strongly. If you are also resisting, you may need to look at what you get out of being sick, or not eating right, or getting enough rest, or not taking care of your emotional needs. If doing for others is your motive in beginning to live a healthier life style, more power to you. However, don't lose sight of the great gift you also give yourself by this approach to living!

Intuition

One of the most connected ways of living occurs when people have the courage to "follow their heart" in making decisions. All of us have heard or felt that small quiet voice inside at some time. My experience has been that when I listen to myself, I make my best decisions. When I ignore my heart's message, I often have gotten in too much of a hurry, or I won't let go of my pride, or I am just not willing to do what I need to do. Inevitably, I find that if I had listened, I would have dealt much more effectively with the situation.

Some people are threatened by the idea of intuition. Rather than understanding it for the strength it is, they are afraid it is somehow weak or silly. They will usually opt to do the "logical" thing, defined as the thing that others would say was safe or made the most sense. They do this rather than having the courage to do what they believe deep inside would be best or would make them happiest. The "pitfall" here is that many people feel more secure in explaining their decisions to others, and to themselves, when their decisions are based on facts alone and not on feelings.

However, there is no conflict between our intellect and our intuition, and they are actually designed to be used together. Our intuition is our *sensitive* side which brings ideas and feelings into our awareness. Our intellect is our *active* side which helps us find ways to express our feelings or to bring our ideas into reality. Using our intuition means learning to think with our mind but decide from our heart.

Intuition is also an extremely important tool in helping. You will frequently find in talking with people that intuition will tell you more than their words are saying. Learning to trust our intuition is one of the greatest strengths and skills helping people can develop. If the thought occurs to us, then it is probably valid to some extent and needs to be checked out with the person. Being willing to act upon our intuition develops deeper connections with ourselves and others.

Projection

It is interesting how we see others and the world. It is not at all unusual for two people to see another person differently or to feel differently about the same circumstances. The reason is that our feelings are subjective rather than objective. We see things as we are, rather than as they are.

People frequently project *their* feelings onto others. For example, a man who accuses his girlfriend of cheating on him, when there is no evidence, often has cheated on her or has been thinking of cheating on her. Or, the girl who has been unjustly criticized by her parents may believe that her friends are also being unjustly criticized whenever they have conflicts with their parents. We often see in other people what *we* feel or think or do rather than what *they* feel or think or do. The "pitfall" for the helper happens when we have not dealt sufficiently with our own issues. Then we will tend to see other people's situations from our own point of view rather than from theirs.

We also tend to project our beliefs onto the world. If we believe that the world is made up of people who will like us and want the best for us, we will be friendly and accepting, and people will like us. However, if we believe that people are going to reject us, we will act cold and aloof, and we will be rejected because we are so unfriendly! People react to our reaction. It is in this way that we create our own reality out of our beliefs.

Fear

Fear is at the base of all the problems we have in how we feel about ourselves, other people, and in how we perceive the world. For example, we are often afraid to try something new because it might not come easily to us, and we will feel like a failure. Or, we are afraid someone might not like us, so we avoid them rather than taking the risk of reaching out. Or, we are afraid to enjoy life because we are always waiting for something to go wrong.

The first thing to realize about fear is that *we* are the ones who give it power. A common reaction to fear is to want to run away from it. However, if we do, we will always be looking back over our shoulder. This holds our fear to us. We give our fear power by allowing it to control us. To take away the power of fear, we need only to turn, face it, and allow it to be there. When we learn to accept and express our fear, knowing that it carries a lesson we need, it will no longer make us afraid.

If we do not learn to do this, we will create the very thing we fear out of our fear. Consider the girl who is afraid that her boyfriend does not really care for her. She thinks that he is going to end up wanting to be with someone else. So, she is always afraid that she will say the wrong thing, and she feels depressed that he doesn't care more for her. Of course, this thinking affects her actions toward him. She becomes withdrawn and unable to relax with him, and she swings between being argumentative and trying too hard to please him. As it turns out, her boyfriend has stronger feelings for her than for any other girl he has ever known, but he has a hard time expressing his feelings. Lately, though, she really seems to have changed, and he can tell that she doesn't feel the same about him. So, he decides that it would probably be best if they stopped seeing each other! Out of fear, she caused the very thing she was afraid would happen.

Or, consider the guy who hates, absolutely hates, speaking before a group. He imagines all sorts of terrible things happening. He imagines that people will laugh at him because he talks weird and acts weird. Because of his thinking, he is miserable and can't even begin to be comfortable in front of a group. He won't look at people, and he turns away from them whenever he can. He expresses himself strangely, mumbling and fumbling most of the time, and some of them decide that he is kind of weird. Out of fear, he caused the very thing he was afraid would happen.

Also, we are often afraid of our own feelings. We are afraid that if we start expressing them, we won't be able to stop. We are afraid that we will lose control, and the feeling will completely take over. However, it actually works in just the opposite way. The more we try to deny a feeling, or to "stuff" it inside, the more likely it is to spill over at the worst possible moment. Again, out of fear, we cause the very thing we are afraid will happen.

In a single day, we make a startling number of choices, and all of our choices are either fear choices or growth choices. We all have reason to learn to recognize the presence and affect that fear has in our lives.

Unconditional Love

When we talk of unconditional love, this does not refer to a romantic type of love in which we are willing to do anything or be anything for another person. Unconditional love does not even necessarily imply that we like a person! It does not mean that we don't notice people's faults or their mistakes anymore. It does not mean that we stop expressing our feelings and needs to others. It does not mean that we stop having opinions, deciding what is valid for us, or making evaluations.

What it does mean is that our evaluations carry no judgments. Unconditional love means being able to see what is, without judging it as good or bad. Unconditional love means acceptance. It means knowing that people are doing the best they can at the present moment even though that is not always the best they know. Unconditional love means understanding that what people do or say or feel is a result of their experiences. Unconditional love means being able to separate the behavior from the person.

While we all enjoy being with people we like, we can actually learn the most from the people we don't like. People are our mirrors. Often, what we see in others that we don't like is something that is true of ourselves. As we learn to accept others more freely, we are able to take a closer look at ourselves and to recognize those things about ourselves that we have pushed out of our awareness.

Being judgmental is something we do in our heads, while being accepting is something we do in our hearts. Who we are is what we do. To discover who we are, we need look no further than what we think and what we do.

Our minds and hearts are truly open when we have learned to let go of all feelings such as jealousy, hatred, revenge, anger, and prejudice and to respond to every person in every situation with unconditional love instead. This is our greatest reason for being and our most important lesson.

Do You "Should" on Yourself? (Or Others?)

Many people live under the tyranny of "should" all their lives. If you recognize yourself in any of the following examples, then you may be "should-ing" on yourself, and others, too.

Example: You run for an office in school or in a club, and you are not elected.

"Should-ing"
"I should have been able to get elected. Since people didn't vote for me, they obviously don't like me and don't think I'd do a good job."

Accepting
"I'm disappointed I didn't get elected. But, I did meet a lot of new people, and now more people know who I am."

Example: You've finally gone out on a date with this great person. You are having dinner at an expensive restaurant. You reach for your glass and spill it all over the table and your date.

"Should-ing"
"What a klutz! I should be smooth and sophisticated. I'm a total reject. No way will my date ever want to go out with me again."

Accepting
"I'm embarrassed. I guess I'm a lot more nervous than I realized. I've looked forward to this evening for so long that I probably put too much pressure on myself."

Example: You volunteer to work with a student who has been having trouble at home and has asked to talk to a peer counselor. However, after 30 minutes, it is becoming obvious that this person is not comfortable talking with you.

"Should-ing"

"I should be able to get anyone to open up since I'm a peer counselor. Since I can't get this person to open up, it probably just shows I'm not going to be any good at this. I'd better stick to working with people I already know."

Accepting

"I would have liked to have this person open up and get rid of some of the pressure. I know how hard that can be to do, though. I'll just make sure it's clear that I care and that I'll be around."

Example: You and your parents are fighting a lot lately. You know down deep that you are a big part of the problem. But, they've done a lot to make things worse, too.

"Should-ing"

*"You should be able to make things better around here without my help. **You're** the parents. It's one thing for me to make mistakes, but you should know better!"*

Accepting

"This must be hard for all of us since no one seems to be handling it well. I can see some things I could do to help. Maybe I'm actually the best one to handle this."

When you "should" on yourself (or others) in this way, you are punishing yourself (or others) for the fact that you (or they) are not perfect. When you are accepting of yourself (or others), you are using life's experiences as lessons for growth.

Unit II
Skills Development

Peer Helping Pre-Test

For each of the statements below, write what you feel would be a helpful response to a person who had made that statement to you:

1. "I really hate this school and this town! I didn't want to move—especially to this place. I can tell this is going to be a lousy year."

2. "I can't believe it! She did it to me again! I told my friend something I didn't want anyone else to know, and now it's all over the school. I'm going to find a way to get even with her."

3. "I just found out that my best friend was killed by a drunk driver last night. And to make things worse, the last time we talked, we had an argument. I was going to try to settle things this weekend."

4. "When my dad drinks, he and my mom start arguing. They have these terrible fights. What should I do?"

5. "I'm failing my English class, and if I don't pass it, I won't graduate. My parents are always on my back about getting good grades so I'll get a scholarship. I think I'm going to lose my job, and now I seem to be fighting with my friends all the time. Sometimes I'm really not sure life is worth it."

Rules of Brainstorming

1. **Express no negative evaluation.** Every idea is accepted. This encourages people to participate freely.

2. **Work for quantity.** Try to get a flow of ideas. Quality is a by-product of quantity.

3. **Expand on each other's ideas.** "Piggy-back" on each other's suggestions. This encourages people to work as a team.

4. **Encourage far-out ideas.** Often a great solution has its beginning in a new and creative way to approach a problem.

5. **Record each idea.** Write down the key word or phrase of every idea suggested so that everyone can see them.

6. **Set a time limit.** Decide on a time limit and stop when time is up. This takes away from the tendency to strive for the perfect solution before stopping.

Chapter 2

Attending Skill

Attending is the first and most fundamental skill of peer helping. Because attending skills are easy to learn, it is also easy to assume they are not as important as some of the more difficult skills we will discuss later in the training. However, all of the other skills you will learn are based upon a mastery of this skill and upon an automatic ability to attend to the other person in a helping relationship. Also, although attending looks and sounds easy, skillful attending is work which requires a high level of energy and concentration.

Lack of attending in relationships is sadly all too common. Think how often you hear people say, "You're not even listening to me!" Usually what has happened is that one person is talking and the other person is listening, but is also glancing around, or looking through a magazine, or staring off into space. Even though the person may have heard every word said, the nonattending behavior has communicated a lack of concern and involvement. It is not enough to listen to people. We must also *look* like we are listening to them.

An interesting example of the power of attending is shown by Ivey and Hinkle (1970). Six students in a psychology class planned an experiment on attending, using their professor as the target. They started class sitting in slouched postures and listening only passively. At a prearranged signal, the students switched to attentive, involved postures using active eye contact with the professor. When *they* changed, the professor changed from using a monotone to using many gestures and facial expressions. A lively exchange and stimulating discussion followed. At another prearranged signal, the students went back to slouching and passive listening. After several futile attempts to reestablish contact, the poor professor slipped back into his old monotone and class ended on that note.

Although I definitely do not recommend that you try this experiment on your advisor or other teachers, it certainly does show the importance of the role the listener plays in any relationship! It also clearly shows that people tend to develop and grow when they feel listened to and to withdraw when they do not.

In attending to others, we use several specific behaviors. Most of these involve using our body posture to communicate availability. Facing the other person squarely is the posture which most clearly shows involvement. In addition, an "open" posture shows that the helper is open to what the other person has to say, as well as being open to that person as someone deserving respect. Crossed arms and legs sometimes signal when people are "closed" to another person or when they are in disagreement with what is being said. Leaning toward the other person is another sign of complete presence and involvement, while leaning away from someone often signals withdrawal or resistance to what is being said.

Good eye contact is another important attending behavior. It involves looking comfortably at another person, but never intruding upon that person by staring. Looking at a person is an important way of demonstrating involvement, but it is also a helpful tool for gathering as much information as possible. People's body language often reflects their feelings more accurately than their words. A great deal of information and understanding can be lost if we do not look at people when they talk. Completely attending to another person involves learning to listen not only with our ears but with our eyes and also our hearts.

Another necessary condition for attending is for the helper to remain relatively relaxed. It is terribly difficult to listen effectively when we are nervous. We have a tendency to interrupt or to jump in too quickly with responses. We may miss what a person is saying because we are worrying about how we are going to respond instead. Also, we will usually end up making the people we are with nervous because they sense how nervous we are. Although it is difficult not to get nervous when we are talking to people for the first time, one thing that helps is to focus completely on them, putting all our concern into how they are feeling. Before we know it, all our nervousness will be gone.

In attending, the helper also uses what are called "minimal encourages to talk." These include such things as nodding the head, saying "um-hmm," and repeating one or two words or asking short questions. These are important ways to encourage people to continue to talk about their feelings, without jumping prematurely into problem-solving.

As you become more skilled at using attending to communicate with other people, you will also find yourself becoming more aware of your attending behaviors. What may happen next is that you will "catch" yourself one day with your arms crossed and leaning away from someone. Being more aware of your physical posture will make you more aware of your emotional posture. Attending to others, as well as to ourselves, is the first step in becoming more effective friends.

Please Hear What I'm Not Saying

Don't be fooled by me.
Don't be fooled by the face I wear,
For I wear a mask, I wear a thousand masks.
Masks that I am afraid to take off.
But none of them are me.
Pretending is an art that's second nature to me.
But don't be fooled.
I give the impression that I am secure,
That all is sunny and unruffled with me,
Within as well as without.
That confidence is my name and coolness my game,
And that I need no one.
Don't believe me.
Please!

My surface may be smooth,
But my surface is my mask.
My ever concealing mask.
Beneath dwells the real me,
In confusion and fear,
In loneliness.

I idly talk with you in the smooth tones of surface chatter.
I tell you everything that's really nothing,
Of what's crying within me.
So, when I'm going through my routine,
Please don't be fooled by what I'm saying.
Please listen carefully,
and try to hear what I'm not saying,
But what I'd like to be able to say.

Each time you're kind, and gentle, and encouraging,
Each time you try to understand because you really care,
My heart begins to grow wings.
Very small, feeble wings,
but wings.

With your sympathy and sensitivity,
and your power of understanding,
You can breathe life into me.
I want you to know how important you are to me.
How you can be a part of the person that is me,
if you choose to.
Please choose to.
Do not pass me by.

It will not be easy for you.
My sense of worthlessness builds strong walls.
The nearer you approach to me,
the blinder I may strike back.
I fight against the very thing I cry out for.
But I am told that love is stronger than strong walls.
This is my only hope.

Who am I, you may wonder?
I am someone you know very well.
I am a hurting member of your family,
I am the person sitting beside you in this room,
I am every person you meet on the street.
Please don't believe my mask.
Please speak to me, share a little of yourself with me.
At least recognize me.
Please.
Because you care.

Author Unknown
Condensed and Revised

Skills Chart

Make a check mark in one of the boxes next to a behavior each time the behavior is demonstrated:

I. Attending Skill

Sits facing the person   ☐ ☐ ☐ ☐ ☐
Maintains good eye contact   ☐ ☐ ☐ ☐ ☐
Maintains open, available posture   ☐ ☐ ☐ ☐ ☐
Appears relaxed   ☐ ☐ ☐ ☐ ☐
Gives encouragement, such as nodding   ☐ ☐ ☐ ☐ ☐
head

Chapter 3

Empathy Skill

The second skill of peer helping is that of empathy. Empathy is probably the single most identifiable skill that is present in effective helpers, no matter what their style, training, or personality. It is a skill that comes from deep inside, and it is what most contributes to the healing that occurs in people when they are with such a person.

Empathy is easily confused with sympathy. Yet their difference is as great as the difference between lightning and a lightning bug. Sympathy is what we give when we feel sorry for people, and it tends to reinforce weakness rather than challenge growth. Sympathy comes from a belief that there is nothing people can do about their situations. Expressions of sympathy usually sound something like, "Poor baby."

Empathy, on the other hand, is the ability to understand another person's feelings as if they were our own, while remembering that they are not our own. Empathy is being able to feel from another person's perspective and to communicate that understanding. An empathic helper responds with compassion and acceptance but also with respect and a belief that people have the ability to deal with their situations.

Empathic responses reflect back to people the essence, or the "heart," of what they have said, but in our own words. When we are able to first accept and then mirror a person's thoughts and feelings, we show by our understanding that the person is not so different from us. One of the fears people have when things are going wrong is that there must be something wrong with them. When someone is able to demonstrate empathy for what they are experiencing, it allows them to move away from that fear into a clearer understanding of their situation.

Empathy responses also allow a helper to respond relatively frequently to people without taking the focus away from them. They give a helper time to gather more information and to come to a deeper understanding of a situation. This serves an important function in helping to guard against the impulse to jump in prematurely with advice or a solution while a person still has feelings and thoughts left unsaid and unexplored.

Following are some examples of empathy responses:

Friend:
"I think I just failed my history test. My boss told me last night that he's not satisfied with my work. And now I see my girlfriend talking to that guy again!"

Helper:
"Sometimes it seems like everything goes wrong at once."

Friend:
"I know I should be making some decisions about next year, and I feel like I should know what I want to do with my life. But I just seem to keep putting things off."

Helper:
"It's scary when you feel you should be doing something, but you don't know what you want to do."

Friend:
"My boyfriend is spending a lot of time with his old girlfriend again. When I asked him about it, he said there wasn't anything to it, but he wouldn't tell me what they talked about either."

Helper:
"It's hard to trust him when he won't help you understand what is going on."

Because empathy is based on understanding, it develops a trust and openness between two people that leads naturally to deeper and more honest responses. As new thoughts and feelings continue to be understood and accepted, people are stimulated to continue their increased self-awareness and self-exploration.

Becoming an Active Listener

It has been said the reason we have two ears and only one mouth is because we were intended to spend twice as much time listening as talking! This is actually a rare trait in people. Good listeners are people others are naturally drawn to because they always feel better after being with them.

Active listening is a powerful tool for change and growth. In learning to use any powerful tool, the user has a definite role and responsibility. Active listeners never just passively absorb the words that are spoken by others. They work to understand, accept, and respond to both the meaning and the feelings of the person speaking. This requires a genuine respect for the worth of all people and an ability to suspend judgment if we have not "walked a mile in their moccasins."

Something very special happens when people are listened to in this way. They begin to listen to themselves more carefully and to become clearer on exactly what they are thinking and feeling. They become free to do this because they are allowed to be themselves and to make of that what they will.

Active listening has no place for such mental behaviors as listening judgmentally, analyzing why a person does something, or mentally arguing with what a person is saying. These only interfere with the listener's ability to hear what is actually being said.

Active listening is a way to convey to people that we are able to see things from their point of view. In active listening, we reach for the total meaning of what is being said, listening for both the feelings and the content, while reflecting these back to the person. We stay focused on the main points, listening for any relevant themes. We listen both to what is being said and what is not being said. We also give our attention to how it is said. Most importantly, we remember that by listening to people, we communicate to them that they are important and their ideas are valid. In doing this, we also communicate that we are people who care.

Listen

When I ask you to listen to me
and you start giving me advice,
you have not done what I ask.

When I ask you to listen to me
and you begin to tell me
why I shouldn't feel that way,
you are trampling on my feelings.

When I ask you to listen to me
and you feel you have to do something
to solve my problems,
you have failed me,
strange as that may seem.

Listen!
All I asked was that you listen,
not talk or do, just hear me.
Advice is cheap.
A quarter will get you
both Dear Abby and Billy Graham
in the same newspaper.
And I can do for myself,
I'm not helpless.
Maybe discouraged and faltering,
but not helpless.

When you do something for me
that I can and need to do for myself,
you contribute to my fear and weakness.

But when you accept as a simple fact
that I do feel what I feel,
no matter how irrational,
then I quit trying to convince you
and can get about the business of understanding
what's behind this irrational feeling.
And when that's clear,
the answers are obvious and I don't need advice.
Irrational feelings make sense
when we understand what's behind them.

So, please listen and just hear me,
and, if you want to talk,
wait a minute for your turn,
and I'll listen to you.

Author Unknown
Revised

Reflection of Feelings and Content

In order to help other people better understand their feelings, it is important for us to have an extensive "feeling vocabulary." In developing this vocabulary, we move out of the "glad, mad, bad, sad" type of responses and into others which show more depth and definition.

Feelings: Levels of Intensity

Happy
(Strong) Ecstatic, Overjoyed, Thrilled
(Medium) Delighted, Gratified, Excited
(Mild) Pleased, Satisfied, Content

Angry
(Strong) Furious, Outraged, Seething
(Medium) Resentful, Exasperated, Irritated
(Mild) Upset, Annoyed, Ticked

Sad
(Strong) Miserable, Crushed, Heartbroken
(Medium) Depressed, Sorrowful, Dejected
(Mild) Down, Glum, Discouraged

Scared
(Strong) Terrified, Horrified, Alarmed
(Medium) Intimidated, Anxious, Startled
(Mild) Nervous, Uneasy, Unsettled

Confused
(Strong) Bewildered, Disconcerted, Vacillating
(Medium) Doubtful, Unsure, Mixed Up
(Mild) Vague, Puzzled, Undecided

In learning to reflect people's feelings, it is important to recognize that this is not used as a way of _telling_ people how they feel. Rather, it is a way of _acknowledging_ what people have said they feel. It is an effective way to let people know that they are understood. Feeling understood usually stimulates people to talk more and to explore their feelings further, and this will generally lead to greater insight.

Part I

To begin the process of learning how to reflect feelings, imagine yourself listening to each of the people quoted below. Write a response that communicates your understanding of their feelings. Select from the feelings listed or choose your own. Also, notice how different responses will occur to you depending on how you imagine the tone of voice.

Example

Friend:
"My best friends are fighting, and they keep trying to get me to take sides."

Helper:
"You feel irritated."

1. **Friend:**
   "Some days my mother acts like I'm not even there."
   Helper:
   You feel _____.

2. **Friend:**
   "I can't seem to get my parents to trust me anymore."
   Helper:
   You feel _____.

3. **Friend:**
   "I finally did it! I made the honor roll."
   Helper:
   You feel _____.

4. **Friend:**
   "My girlfriend just broke up with me."
   Helper:
   You feel _____.

5. **Friend:**
   "When my parents find out I have been cutting first hour, they are going be furious."
   Helper:
   You feel _____.

Part II

In this section, we will take the process one step further. The most complete response is one that communicates understanding of both the *feelings* being expressed and the *content* of what has been said. We show people by our responses that we understand both their feelings and their reasons for those feelings. Again, imagine yourself listening to someone making the statements written below. This time, show by your response that you understand both the feelings and the content of what has been said.

Example

Friend:
"I don't know if I should talk about it. My family says what happens at home is private. And you and I have never really talked like this before."

Helper:
"You feel confused about whether it's okay to talk because of what your family says and because we haven't been that close before."

1. **Friend:**
   "I thought he was going to kick me out of class for sure. Instead, he called me into his office, and we talked out our differences."
   Helper:
   You feel _____ because _____

2. **Friend:**
   "I can't quite figure him out. I can't tell if he really cares about me or is just using me to make Susan jealous."
   Helper:
   You feel _____ because _____

3. **Friend:**
   "Everybody makes fun of my clothes. My family can't afford to buy me anything new. People don't have to like me, but I wish they would stop making fun of me."
   Helper:
   You feel _____ because _____

4. Friend:
"I have a report due tomorrow. I have to work late tonight. The house is a mess, and my parents are coming home tomorrow."
Helper:
You feel _____ because _____

5. Friend:
"I had the best practices this week! Coach kept telling me what a good job I was doing. And now, I find out I'm not even starting in the game tomorrow."
Helper:
You feel _____ because _____

Part III

In this section, we will take the final step in the process of learning to reflect feelings and content. We now need to look at some other ways of responding, ways that feel more natural. If we *always* responded in the style you have been using in these exercises, we would all sound the same, and people would wonder whether we were genuine. This time, go back to your responses to the last five statements and rephrase them by putting them into your own language and style. Be sure that your response continues to show an understanding of both feelings and content.

Example

Friend:
"I don't know if I should talk about it. My family says what happens at home is private. And you and I have never really talked like this before."

Helper:
"It can be really confusing when you want to talk about something, but you're not sure it's okay. It's even harder for you since we haven't spent much time together."

A Student's Saga

You are at registration with a large group of students who are either waiting to change their schedule or to select their classes for the coming year. People are sitting in chairs, on benches, or on the floor. The line is moving very slowly. Most of the students are laughing, talking, and enjoying seeing their friends again. The person next to you is visibly upset, though. When he turns to you and starts talking, you decide to use your new empathy skills:

"Man, this stinks!" (or other equivalent term)

Your response:

"Those people act like they think we'll sit here all day."

Your response:

"I didn't want to move here in the first place."

Your response:

"The kids at this school look like they'd never notice someone new."

Your response:

"My friends back home are probably all doing something together right now."

Your response:

"This would never have happened if my folks could just get along."

Your response:

"It's like they don't know how to do anything together but fight."

Your response:

"Yeah, and that was bad enough, but then the next thing I hear is that I have to move here with my mom."

Your response:

"I'll be graduating in a year. I don't know why I couldn't decide for myself where I would live."

Your response:

"They say this is a better school and things will be better for me here! How do they know?"

Your response:

"I have to admit I'll probably get into a better college from this school... and sometimes my dad does drink a little too much...."

Your response:

"I know my mom's been real worried about me lately, but I just haven't wanted to talk to her."

Your response:

"I think I've made things a lot harder for both of us."

Your response:

"You know, if everyone here is as understanding as you, I'm really going to like this place. Would you introduce me to some of these people?"

An Exercise in Self-Disclosure

In your work with others, you will be encouraging them to be open about their feelings and life experiences. It is important we never ask others to do what we are not willing to do. A healthy recognition that we all have areas of our lives that could be improved is necessary to avoid feelings of superiority or embarrassment in our work with others.

Your training is a very special opportunity to know and be known by a group of accepting, caring individuals. To become known to others, you will need to be open about feelings or experiences that have made an impact on the person you are today. Your work in Training Triads is an excellent time to do this. When you take the role of friend, instead of using a role play topic, you can choose to talk about actual issues in your life. Besides the personal good feelings and support that this will bring to you, it will also help you to better understand what it feels like to receive help, rather than to give it.

This exercise is designed as an opportunity for you to identify those feelings and experiences that you would like to talk about during Training Triads. As rapport develops within the group and as you learn to trust each other's developing skills, you may find that you will want to add to this list periodically.

Some examples of possible topics are listed below. These are provided as a stimulus in your thinking about possible feelings, situations, or personal characteristics that you would like to discuss. After reading through these examples, please list some of your areas of desired personal development.

Examples

"I'm shy. It's hard for me to meet new people and to be open with them."

"I need to be liked. How I feel about myself depends on how other people feel about me."

"My parents are getting a divorce."

"It's hard for me to stand up for what I believe. Sometimes I just go along."

"The only time I feel good about myself is when I am helping someone else."

"My dad/mom/brother/sister is an alcoholic."

Training Triad Topics:

1.

2.

3.

4.

5.

6.

7.

Skills Chart

Make a check mark in one of the boxes next to a behavior each time the behavior is demonstrated:

I. Attending Skill

Sits facing the person	☐ ☐ ☐ ☐ ☐
Maintains good eye contact	☐ ☐ ☐ ☐ ☐
Maintains open, available posture	☐ ☐ ☐ ☐ ☐
Appears relaxed	☐ ☐ ☐ ☐ ☐
Gives encouragement, such as nodding head	☐ ☐ ☐ ☐ ☐

II. Empathy Skill

Reflects feelings, using different words	☐ ☐ ☐ ☐ ☐
Reflects content, using different words	☐ ☐ ☐ ☐ ☐

Chapter 4
Clarifying/Questioning Skill

The third skill of peer helping is that of clarifying/questioning. This skill is one that many people feel they already have mastered because they use it so often. However, the skill of clarifying/questioning is probably both the most frequently used and the most frequently misused of all the skills we will discuss during your training.

Clarifying statements or questions are a natural part of any conversation in which both people are involved and interested. When we aren't sure we understand what someone else is saying, we will usually ask clarifying questions or make clarifying statements. Some examples are:

> *"Are you saying that...?"*
> *"What you are saying is...."*
> *"Do you mean...?"*

However, it is also important to be aware of some of the other purposes that clarifying statements or questions can serve. One is that they are another good way to signal the other person that we are actively following the conversation and are working to understand. Also, clarifying statements or questions can be used to highlight important thoughts and feelings that have been expressed in the conversation. This sometimes helps people to pause and think more deeply about a situation and their response to it.

Questioning is one of the most common forms of communication and is probably the one that is most overused and misused. Questioning is a skill that few people ever master. Effective questioning can allow a person or relationship to open and grow, just as ineffective questioning can cause a person to withdraw or a relationship to close down. Frequently, the problem with questions is that we ask too many of them, and we don't actually listen to the answers in between. Before long, people feel like they are part of an interrogation rather than a dialogue.

One of the reasons for this is that questions are often really statements in disguise. If I say, "You really didn't like what he said to you, did you?" I have already decided what the answer will be. I might better express myself and encourage you to open up by saying, "If he had said that to me, I would be hurt. How did you feel?" Or, if I say, "Are you angry with me?" and you are only feeling tired, then you feel you have to explain, and possibly defend, how you are feeling. I could more effectively have opened the subject by observing, "You seem quiet today."

When we choose to use questions in our conversations, we need to consider which kind of question is most appropriate. There are really only two kinds of questions. The open question allows people to express themselves in an individual way, often providing unexpected information. The closed question has only the expectation of a "yes" or "no" answer and, as a result, gains very little information.

Open questions, although they do not guarantee a complete answer, at least offer the invitation and opportunity to talk. They typically begin with words like "what," "how," "why," or "would."

> *"What would you like to do about this?"*
> *"How are you feeling?"*
> *"Why do you want to be a peer counselor?"*
> *"Would you tell me more about your family?"*

"Why" questions, especially ones such as, "Why did you do that?" need to be used sparingly as they usually only succeed in making a person feel defensive. People often do not realize why they did something until they have had a chance to sort through their feelings. Of course, it is the way a person is asked "Why?" or any other question for that matter, that determines the outcome. "Why" questions often can be effectively replaced by "What" questions. Instead of "Why did you do that?" we can ask, "What were you feeling when you did that?" or "What were you hoping would happen if you did that?"

Closed questions do have a purpose, of course, when there is factual information we need to know. They typically begin with words like "is," "are," "do," or "did."

> *"Is it my turn?"*
> *"Are you going to work today?"*
> *"Do you mind if I have another piece of pie?"*
> *"Did you call the doctor?"*

Sometimes a closed question will be met by a full and complete answer if the person being asked is outgoing or already feels like talking. On the other hand, an open question can be met with a short, incomplete answer if the person does not want to talk. However, we can certainly improve our chances of initiating a meaningful conversation with another person by our effective use of questions.

Closed:
"Do you like school?"
Open:
"What is your favorite part of school?"

Closed:
"Are you embarrassed?"
Open:
"How do you feel?"

Closed:
"Is this the way you want things to be with us?"
Open:
"What kind of relationship do you want for us?"

Some Clarifying Questions

Good clarifying questions can be used to deepen our understanding of what is being said or to allow people to consider a situation and their feelings about it more deeply. Try one of these in your next conversation:

1. How important is that to you?
2. What is another choice you have?
3. How did you feel when that happened?
4. What did you do when he or she did that?
5. Are you glad about that?
6. What are your reasons for saying that?
7. Was that your choice?
8. What would you like to have happen?
9. Can you give me an example?
10. What would happen if you did that?
11. Can you tell me what you mean by that?
12. What is your next step?
13. If you had it to do over, would you do it the same way?
14. What are some good things about that?
15. Can you do anything about that?
16. What would have to happen for things to work out that way?
17. How long have you felt this way?
18. What makes that hard for you?
19. Is that how you feel or what you have been told?
20. What would you tell your best friend to do about that?

Skills Chart

Make a check mark in one of the boxes next to a behavior each time the behavior is demonstrated:

I. Attending Skill

Sits facing the person ☐ ☐ ☐ ☐ ☐
Maintains good eye contact ☐ ☐ ☐ ☐ ☐
Maintains open, available posture ☐ ☐ ☐ ☐ ☐
Appears relaxed ☐ ☐ ☐ ☐ ☐
Gives encouragement, such as nodding ☐ ☐ ☐ ☐ ☐
head

II. Empathy Skill

Reflects feelings, using different words ☐ ☐ ☐ ☐ ☐
Reflects content, using different words ☐ ☐ ☐ ☐ ☐

III. Clarifying/Questioning Skill

Uses clarifying questions or statements ☐ ☐ ☐ ☐ ☐
Asks open questions ☐ ☐ ☐ ☐ ☐
Asks closed questions ☐ ☐ ☐ ☐ ☐

Chapter 5

Assertiveness Skill

The fourth skill of peer helping is that of assertiveness. When many females think of assertiveness, they imagine a pushy, bristly sort of person. When many males think of assertiveness, they picture a weak, whining sort of person. This comes largely from the way our culture has conditioned us to respond, depending on our sex. Females receive many messages that they are to be pleasing, giving, and pacifying. Males receive just as many messages that they are to be strong and aggressive, doing whatever is necessary to achieve their goals. In a broad and general sense, male and female behaviors often represent opposite ends of the behavior spectrum. The conditioned female response can be seen as representing the passive end of the spectrum while the conditioned male response can be seen as representing the aggressive end of the spectrum.

Assertiveness can be seen as the middle response in the behavior spectrum. In being assertive, we take care of our needs and self-esteem, while recognizing that the needs of others are equally important. When we respond aggressively, we again take care of our needs, but this time we do it at the expense of others. When we respond passively, we take care of the needs of others, but we violate our own needs in the process.

Aggressiveness is often followed by a momentary rush, kind of a "gotcha" feeling. However, this usually is followed by feelings of uneasiness or guilt which in turn lead to lowered self-esteem. After an aggressive act, a person will often look to others for support and justification. On the other hand, passiveness usually is followed by feelings of resentment. Unconsciously, a person often will seek revenge in little ways, such as by "forgetting," being late, or "not understanding." However, this too leads to feelings of lowered self-esteem. Both passive and aggressive behaviors stem from feelings of low self-esteem and generate new feelings of low self-esteem.

Most of us have responded in each of these three styles at some time in our lives. However, we all tend to have a predominant style of relating to the world. In learning to be more assertive, it is important to remember that when we begin to act differently, we begin to feel differently. Any time we want to feel differently, we only need to behave differently! We can raise our self-esteem by choosing behaviors which make us feel good about ourselves.

Assertiveness is a way of expressing ourselves that is open and honest, but also caring. Through assertiveness, we can learn to express even strong feelings in such a way that we are able to maintain, and often improve, our relationships. When conflicts arise, they are much more likely to be resolved satisfactorily when we respond assertively.

Out of a fear of expressing negative emotions, people tend to bottle up their feelings until they can no longer stand it. Then, they let out all their accumulated frustration, resentment, and anger at one time, "dumping" all over people. Then they feel bad and decide that the problem is in ever telling anyone how they feel. This sets up a vicious cycle of repressing feelings until they can't be repressed anymore, finally exploding, feeling guilty, working harder to repress feelings, and on and on. They do this because they have not yet realized that it is *how* we express ourselves that makes the difference.

There are hundreds of examples of this in our daily lives. For instance, if your older brother is so loud that you cannot hear the person you are talking with on the telephone, you can sit and seethe and say nothing (passive). Or, you can say nothing for as long as you can stand it and then yell at him to "Shut up!" (aggressive). Or, you can tell him how you feel about his actions and why it is important to you (assertive). "I'm really frustrated at how hard it is to hear with all the noise you are making! I have looked forward to this phone call all day."

This way of communicating is called an "I" message, and it is an important technique in learning to communicate assertively. Although an "I" message does not guarantee a change in the other person's behavior, it does greatly increase our chances. Most people respond well when others express their feelings sincerely and with respect. You will find, though, that some people become angry and threatened when others deal with them assertively. Ironically, although people will usually agree that being assertive is the only way to be, they don't always mean *with them*! It is important at those times to remember that a person's response is their responsibility, not ours. *Not* dealing with others assertively usually only leads to more and worse problems later.

An "I" message generally consists of three parts. The first part of the "I" message describes *how you feel* as a result of someone's behavior. When you take responsibility for your feelings and are willing to state what they are, you provide important information for the relationship. Misunderstandings can be cleared up, and new information about each person's needs can be shared. This is an important opportunity for both people to look closer at the situation and their feelings as a way of deepening understanding.

The second part of the "I" message describes *the person's behavior specifically*. For example, it is generally not very helpful to tell people that they are "inconsiderate slobs." A much more responsible statement would be, "This is the second time this week I have had to clean our apartment."

The more specific you can be in describing the behavior that is causing the problem, the more likely it is that a person will decide to change the behavior.

The third, and last, part of the "I" message gives *an explanation for the feelings* or explains the consequences of the offending behavior. This statement communicates to the other person why it is important to you that the behavior be changed. In this way, you help others to understand you better by talking about the things that are important to you.

Here are some examples of "I" messages:

> *"I feel embarrassed when you put me down in front of people because it seems like you don't want them to respect me."*

> *"I feel angry when you don't call when you say you are going to because it makes me think that our relationship isn't important to you."*

> *"I feel hurt when you make fun of me for being overweight because I have explained to you how bad I start to feel about myself."*

"I" messages are an excellent way to share feelings of all kinds. They can be used to share appreciation and to give positive feedback as well as to express needs. Because the complete "I" message gives a great deal of information to another person, it requires openness and a sense of value as a person. In our intimate relationships, it requires a courage that is born of knowing that the only way to be close to another person is to let that person know who we are.

Sometimes using an "I" message solves the problem by itself. For one thing, when we work to phrase our feelings in an "I" message, we often end up clarifying things for ourselves as well. At other times, it simply opens up the lines of communication and awareness between two people. This is what has usually been lost when two people are no longer in harmony with each other.

Assess Your Assertiveness

To discover how assertive you are in your own personal life, draw a circle around the number that best describes your typical response to the situations given. Most people find that their most honest response is usually the first response that occurs to them.

Key: 0-Never 1-Sometimes 2-Usually 3-Always

0 1 2 3   1. Do you find it easy to talk to someone you don't already know?

0 1 2 3   2. When a friend asks a favor that is unreasonable, do you say no?

0 1 2 3   3. Do you find that name-calling is a good way to win arguments?

0 1 2 3   4. If you disagree with something being said in class, do you say so?

0 1 2 3   5. On a date, are you comfortable if there is a lull in the conversation?

0 1 2 3   6. At a restaurant, do you find it easy to decide what to order?

0 1 2 3   7. If someone cuts in line ahead of you, do you object?

0 1 2 3   8. Do you find that the best defense is a good offense?

0 1 2 3   9. If friends borrow money and forget to repay you, do you remind them?

0 1 2 3   10. Do you look at people when you talk to them?

0 1 2 3   11. If you feel you have been treated unfairly by a parent or teacher, do you say so?

0 1 2 3   12. Do you refuse to go along with the crowd when you think what they are doing is wrong?

0   1   2   3   13. If friends say things to put you down, do you let them know how you feel?

0   1   2   3   14. Do you like to continue an argument after the other person wants to stop?

0   1   2   3   15. If your date pushes you to do something you don't want to do, are you able to say no clearly?

0   1   2   3   16. Do you avoid laughing at jokes that you think are in bad taste?

0   1   2   3   17. If someone is rude to you, are you rude back?

0   1   2   3   18. When someone pays you a compliment, do you know what to say?

0   1   2   3   19. If you have plans with a friend, and he or she changes them at the last minute to accept a date, do you speak up?

0   1   2   3   20. Do you object if a friend or date drives too fast?

0   1   2   3   21. How often do you tell your deepest feelings to someone you trust?

0   1   2   3   22. When you disagree with others, do you find that you are always right?

0   1   2   3   23. If you feel a teacher has miscalculated your grade, do you discuss it with him or her?

0   1   2   3   24. Do you ever ask others for help?

0   1   2   3   25. Are you able to praise others?

0   1   2   3   26. If people can't decide what they want, do you think it's helpful to make decisions for them?

0   1   2   3   27. If someone harasses you, do you stand up for yourself?

0 1 2 3 28. Do you feel it's better to express your-self, even if someone might object, than to keep quiet about something that is bothering you?

0 1 2 3 29. Are you able to relax when giving a pre-sentation in class or before a group?

0 1 2 3 30. Do you find a way to get what you want in any situation?

0 1 2 3 31. If your boss asks you to stay late or come in early without paying you extra, do you discuss it with him or her?

0 1 2 3 32. If you buy a new shirt that comes apart in the wash, do you return it for a re-fund?

0 1 2 3 33. Do you ever criticize something a friend does that you think is wrong?

0 1 2 3 34. Are you able to openly express affec-tion or appreciation?

0 1 2 3 35. Are you openly critical of other peo-ple's opinions when you disagree?

0 1 2 3 36. If you don't have someone to eat lunch with, do you ask to join a group of peo-ple?

0 1 2 3 37. If people ask if you mind if they smoke, and you do, do you say so?

0 1 2 3 38. Do you invite others to do things rather than waiting to be asked?

0 1 2 3 39. At a party, if things start happening that you don't like, do you leave?

0 1 2 3 40. If all your friends don't like someone, but you do, do you speak to that person anyway?

0 1 2 3 41. Do you stick to your goals even when others put them down?

Scoring

A. ADD your responses for questions: 1, 2, 4, 5, 6, 7, 9, 10, 11, 12, 13, 15, 16, 18, 19, 20, 21, 23, 24, 25, 27, 28, 29, 31, 32, 33, 34, 36, 37, 38, 39, 40, 41
"A" TOTAL _____

B. ADD your responses for questions: 3, 8, 14, 17, 22, 26, 30, 35
"B" TOTAL _____

C. SUBTRACT: "B" TOTAL from "A" TOTAL
SCORE _____

If your score is 67-99, you are exceptionally assertive, expressing your feelings appropriately in a variety of situations.

If your score is 34-66, you are frequently assertive while perhaps needing to push yourself to express your feelings more freely or more appropriately in some situations.

If your score is 0-33, you are rarely assertive and are probably experiencing dissatisfaction in your personal and social relationships.

"I" Messages:
Learning to Speak Assertively

Language is incredibly powerful. The words that we use in our minds or in our speech will largely determine how we think. How we think affects how we feel and determines how we act. In learning to take complete responsibility for our feelings, we can begin by focusing on our language and style of communication.

An "I" message, which is an assertive response, is an excellent tool for honest, helpful communication. It requires us to focus on our feelings, taking responsibility for choosing to feel that way. The opposite of an "I" message is a "You" message, and it is usually an aggressive response.

A "You" message is used to switch the focus to the other person, shifting responsibility for our situation or feelings onto that person. With "You" messages, we blame others for what we are experiencing, rather than acknowledging our responsibility and power in determining the situation. A "You" message also effectively gives no information about ourselves while making many assumptions about the other person. "You" messages tend to bring out feelings of defensiveness or guilt in another person. They usually either end the exchange of thoughts and feelings, or they begin an exchange of negative, blaming accusations.

"I" messages, on the other hand, are helpful in bringing about an exchange of positive expectation and trust. They represent a belief that people will want to do something about a situation if they have the information needed to better understand. For this reason, "I" messages are most commonly observed in open, healthy, and developing relationships.

To begin the process of speaking more assertively, we will use the following model for phrasing an "I" message:

I feel _____ when you _____
because I _____

Part I

Give a "You" message and an "I" message for each of the following situations:

Example

Situation:
Your boss gives you a low rating on your job evaluation which means you won't be considered for a promotion to manager.

"You" message:
"You have never liked me and are always looking for a way to get me!"

"I" message:
"I feel disappointed and surprised that you gave me such a low evaluation because I thought you were happy with my work."

1. Situation:
    Your best friend brags a lot when you are with other people, and it makes you uncomfortable.

    "You" message:

    "I" message:
    *I feel _____ when you _____
    because I _____*

2. Situation:
    A person you have just started working with as a peer counselor tells you that you aren't helping and don't know what you are doing.

    "You" message:

    "I" message:
    *I feel _____ when you _____
    because I _____*

3. Situation:
   As soon as you get on the phone each night, your father decides he needs to use the phone, or he wants you to do something.

   "You" message:

   "I" message:
   I feel _____ *when you* _____
   because I _____

4. Situation:
   You and your brother share the use of the family car. You made arrangements with him to use it tonight, and he is supposed to have it home by 7:00 p.m. He arrives home at 7:25 p.m.

   "You" message:

   "I" message:
   I feel _____ *when you* _____
   because I _____

5. Situation:
   Your girlfriend/boyfriend flirts with other people whenever you are not around. Other people make sure you hear about it.

   "You" message:

   "I" message:
   I feel _____ *when you* _____
   because I _____

Part II

Now that you have a feel for the information that needs to be included in an "I" message, let's work at incorporating that information in your own style of speaking.

Go back to your "I" message responses to each of the five situations and rewrite them by putting them into your own language. Be sure that you include the three elements of an "I" message: how you feel, as a result of what behavior, and why it is important to you.

Example

Situation:
Your boss gives you a low rating on your job evaluation which means you won't be considered for a promotion to manager.

> **"I" message:**
> *"I am really surprised by the job evaluation I received from you. I feel good about the work I am doing, and I thought you did, too. I would like to discuss what I am doing wrong because one of my goals is to be manager someday."*

1. Situation:
   Your best friend brags a lot when you are with other people, and it makes you uncomfortable.

   "I" message:

2. Situation:
   A person you have just started working with as a peer counselor tells you that you aren't helping and don't know what you are doing.

   "I" message:

3. Situation:
   As soon as you get on the phone each night, your father decides he needs to use the phone, or he wants you to do something.

   "I" message:

4. Situation:
   You and your brother share the use of the family car. You made arrangements with him to use it tonight, and he is supposed to have it home by 7:00 p.m. He arrives home at 7:25 p.m.

   "I" message:

5. Situation:
   Your girlfriend/boyfriend flirts with other people whenever you are not around. Other people make sure you hear about it.

   "I" message:

Styles of Interaction:
Passive, Assertive, and Aggressive

Goal
Passive: Avoid conflict
Assertive: Solve problems
Aggressive: Win or dominate

Basic Message
Passive: I am not important
Assertive: We are both important
Aggressive: You are not important

Self-Esteem
Passive: Low
Assertive: High
Aggressive: Low

Communication
Passive: Indirect, hinting, dishonest
Assertive: Direct, honest, responsible
Aggressive: Direct, manipulative, abusive

Problem-Solving
Passive: Problems are avoided
Assertive: Problems are attacked
Aggressive: People are attacked

Success Styles
Passive: I was lucky
Assertive: I earned it
Aggressive: I beat everyone

Reaction of Self to the Behavior
Passive: Disgust, no respect for self
Assertive: Confident, respect for self
Aggressive: Righteous at first, guilty later

Reaction of Others to the Behavior
Passive: Frustration, disgust, pity
Assertive: Respect, cooperation, admiration
Aggressive: Resistance, anger, revenge

The Body Language of Assertive Behavior

Handshake. A firm handshake demonstrates confidence and warmth. A limp handshake usually reflects a lack of confidence. A handshake that is too hard is usually a power play.

Body Posture. Face people and display openness, involvement, and confidence. Sit if people are sitting and stand if they are standing. Being on the same level physically signifies being equal in other respects.

Eye Contact. Look at people as you speak using natural, comfortable eye contact. Never allow it to become rigid. Watch that you do not end eye contact when you disagree with what the other person says.

Active Listening. A person who demonstrates active listening also demonstrates the confidence to hear and deal with whatever another person has to say. However, a person who either refuses to listen or cannot seem to understand what is being said demonstrates insecurity and a closed mind.

Personal Space. Recognize that most people have a personal space of about an arm's length around them. Stand or sit appropriately close without violating or exaggerating this space.

Facial Expression. Make sure your facial expression matches your words. If you tell people you are angry, don't smile! If you are expressing appreciation, don't frown!

Voice. A well-modulated voice reflects a calm and confident emotional state. A voice that is too loud often shows a loss of control. A voice that is too soft often shows a feeling of unimportance. A sarcastic tone is sure to get a less than desired result!

Hand Gestures. Gestures which are natural add emphasis to a message. Over emphatic gestures are usually a sign of aggressiveness. Fidgeting or fiddling with objects usually communicates a lack of confidence.

An Exercise in Developing Assertiveness

1. List several small, less important areas in your life in which you could benefit from being more assertive. Begin practicing these now in preparation for being more assertive in the more important areas of your life.

2. Describe an important situation which occurred recently in which you are not happy with how you responded. Choose a situation which is representative of others that happen frequently and is one in which you would like to respond more assertively.

3. List all of your reasons (rationalizations) for not being assertive in this situation.

4. Decide what it is that you fear. Ask yourself what is the worst that can happen. Examine your behavior and look at the likely consequences. Also examine your self-talk.

5. Describe the general patterns in the situation. Look for the Who, What, Where, and When's.

6. Imagine yourself responding assertively and handling the situation in a totally successful way, feeling confident and respectful of both yourself and the other person. Describe that situation as if it is happening now.

Skills Chart

Make a check mark in one of the boxes next to a behavior each time the behavior is demonstrated:

I. Attending Skill

Sits facing the person ☐ ☐ ☐ ☐ ☐
Maintains good eye contact ☐ ☐ ☐ ☐ ☐
Maintains open, available posture ☐ ☐ ☐ ☐ ☐
Appears relaxed ☐ ☐ ☐ ☐ ☐
Gives encouragement, such as nodding ☐ ☐ ☐ ☐ ☐
head

II. Empathy Skill

Reflects feelings, using different words ☐ ☐ ☐ ☐ ☐
Reflects content, using different words ☐ ☐ ☐ ☐ ☐

III. Clarifying/Questioning Skill

Uses clarifying questions or statements ☐ ☐ ☐ ☐ ☐
Asks open questions ☐ ☐ ☐ ☐ ☐
Asks closed questions ☐ ☐ ☐ ☐ ☐

IV. Assertiveness Skill

Uses "I" messages ☐ ☐ ☐ ☐ ☐
Uses "You" messages ☐ ☐ ☐ ☐ ☐

Chapter 6
Confrontation Skill

Confrontation is the fifth skill of peer helping. Confrontation is an extremely loaded word for many people, conjuring up images of overwhelming emotional wreckage. These people approach even the idea of confrontation by doing what is called "catastrophizing." That is, they imagine that the absolutely worst possible catastrophe will happen if they confront someone. Unfortunately, they use "catastrophizing" to talk themselves out of all confrontations.

Most of us do have good reasons for feeling apprehensive about using confrontation. We have probably all had the experience of confronting someone who did not receive the information well at all! Perhaps the experience became more of a "blow-up" than a confrontation, and we were left with the feeling that things were worse than before.

There are at least two possible explanations for this. It may have been that the person who was being confronted was simply not willing to accept this new information. Or, perhaps not knowing the guidelines for effective confrontation, we may not have handled the situation as well as we could. It is at times like these we have to remember our experiences are opportunities for learning. The wise person is the one who uses them to add to the storehouse of knowledge, rather than to eliminate experiences.

Confrontation is a blending of assertiveness principles with an understanding of the importance of timing and commitment. Confrontation occurs in all healthy relationships and is the test of the relationship. Even though confrontation does tend to unsettle things for awhile, the relationship that endures and emerges has an added depth. One of the fastest ways to recognize a relationship in trouble is to see that no one cares enough or has courage enough to deal with any issues that could lead to disagreement. Growth is the sign of life, and anything not growing is dying.

It is important to approach confrontation with realistic expectations. Too often, we judge the value of confrontation by whether the outcome is positive. Even though it is true that a confrontation well executed increases our chances of success, there are so many variables that we are better off focusing on the process, rather than the outcome. The most important reason for using confrontation is to protect our personal integrity and self-esteem. If we also achieve a positive outcome, we have reason to celebrate and to acknowledge the strength of the relationship. If the outcome is not as positive as we had hoped, we still have accomplished our goal of expressing our needs in the relationship. If a relationship cannot survive an honest but caring expression of feelings, it was a relationship built on illusion, guaranteed to bring unhappiness in the long run.

Here are some guidelines for effective confrontation:

Commitment to the relationship. The decision to confront needs to be based on a commitment to an on-going relationship with the person being confronted. Otherwise, it is probably just an excuse to ventilate feelings or to displace anger.

Timing. Probably the single most critical factor in a successful confrontation is timing. However, we need to remember that there is no such thing as the perfect time for confrontation! If we wait for the perfect time, we will probably end up "stockpiling and dumping." A confrontation needs to come as close to the event as possible. If there *is* an ideal time, it is probably when things are going well. But then we say to ourselves, "Why spoil things? Everything is going so well. Maybe it won't happen anymore." However, when people are feeling positive, they are also feeling strong and can better assimilate what we have to say.

Calm, gentle tone of voice. Because the words of a confrontation are powerful, the tone in which they are said needs to be gentle in order not to overwhelm a person. This means, of course, that a confrontation should never be done while angry.

Know what you want to say. Plan what you are going to say so that you can focus on what you want the person to understand. Be precise, concise, and use examples. Talk about your feelings of loss and make a clear statement of what you hope will happen. The trap in not planning what we will say is that we tend to get sidetracked and may spend the entire time simply expressing negative feelings. Never allow yourself to strip away a person's dignity by how you choose to express yourself.

Set a time. After letting people know that you have something you need to discuss, allow them to help choose when the discussion will occur. We must remember that we have spent time getting ready for a confrontation, and the other person has had no time to prepare for being on the receiving end. Allow people to say if they are not up to it right now, if that is the case, and be willing to defer to the next day. Be sensitive without allowing yourself to be manipulated.

In private. Always ensure privacy for the person that you are confronting. Only those directly involved in the situation have any reason to be included. You will go a long way toward setting up positive conditions for yourself if you see to it that the other person is not put in an unnecessarily defensive position.

Listen. Understand that a person may have some shocked or defensive reactions to work through before being able to proceed effectively with the discussion. Also, be alert to any new information that gives you a different perspective or better understanding of the situation. Listen closely for any expression of needs from the other person.

Work to reach a shared solution. Decide together what you have learned about each other that you had not realized earlier. Acknowledge any areas of misunderstanding. Make a clear and specific statement of what each of you will do differently and what you hope to accomplish by doing it.

Unresolved conflicts have probably undermined more relationships than any other single factor. However, when we master the skill of confrontation, we have in our possession another powerful tool that can be used to create a more positive environment for ourselves and others. We begin to feel better about ourselves, others, and the world in general. We also learn that how we experience the world is our responsibility and is within our control.

I Will Do You No Favor

If I withhold
my voice of anger from you
for your sake,
You, in listening too hard to me,
will hear more anger
than ever any real voice of mine
would have held.

All that I withhold
diminishes me
and cheats you.
All that you withhold
diminishes you
and cheats me.
When we hold back ourselves
for each other's sake,
That is no service
to us either one.
We only conspire
in the weakening of us both.

Author Unknown
Condensed and Revised

Rules for Fighting Fair:
Because All is NOT Fair in Love and War

Avoid name-calling. One of the fastest ways to cause a person to feel humiliated and want to return the favor is to use name-calling or other hostile language. Not only is it demeaning, it also communicates a total lack of respect, which must be present if a relationship is to survive and grow. Finger pointing and other aggressive behaviors are just another form of name-calling using body language.

Avoid generalizations. Nothing in human behavior is "never" or "always" true. Avoid statements such as "You never think of anyone else!" or "You always ruin everything!" Be specific in your language and give examples to help the other person understand your concern.

Avoid comparisons. It is faulty thinking to compare one human being to another. We are all different, and we have a right to expect that our differences will be accepted. Although comparisons of this kind occur in many relationships, the worst abuses of this occur in families where brothers and sisters are compared with each other.

Avoid the "stockpiling/dumping" cycle. It is a sure sign that this is happening when a person says, "And furthermore...." Deal with one issue at a time and do it as close as possible to the event.

Avoid asking "why." Rather than asking people why they did something, simply express how you feel about what happened. Asking "why" is usually a rather effective device for reminding people of their inadequacies.

Avoid interruptions. One of the best ways to contribute to misunderstanding is to interrupt people before they have had an opportunity to complete their statements.

Avoid random fighting. If you find that the situation has deteriorated to the point that you are fighting regularly and at random, make an appointment to fight with each other. This prevents negative habits such as continual nagging or fault finding from developing. It also builds in periods of neutrality.

Own your feelings. Never let the heat of the moment convince you that your feelings are someone else's responsibility. Say "I am angry" not "You make me angry!" Check out your assumptions about other people's feelings. Just because you have known people for a long time does not mean you know what they are thinking or feeling at the time.

Take responsibility for change. It is a rare situation indeed when the responsibility lies with only one person. There are two sides, or more, to every situation. We all contribute to the development of a problem in our own way.

Develop signals. Agree in advance on mutually respected signals which can be used to alert the other person that a problem behavior is developing. For example, you can agree to raise your right hand as a signal each time someone interrupts. Signals allow people to take care of their needs in the discussion without resorting to walking away or other disruptive behavior. Thoroughly understand what the signals mean. For example, if people signal "T" for Time Out, know it means they have reached their limit for the present time and that you will decide together when the conversation will resume.

Know the issue. Be sure you know what you are fighting for or about. Ask yourselves if the fight is about the presented issue or if there is an underlying issue. In couple relationships in particular, fights are frequently over something other than the stated issue.

Know what you hope to achieve. People can frequently give a long list of the things they want someone to *stop* doing without being able to name one thing they want the person to *start* doing! Be prepared to suggest a new way of relating to each other.

Helper Confrontation

In addition to learning to use confrontation in our own personal relationships, we also need to know how to use confrontation in our helping relationships. In a helper confrontation, we point out discrepancies in others' behavior that we believe are causing *them* a problem. In a personal confrontation, we point out discrepancies in a person's behavior that are causing *us* a problem.

In helper confrontation, we must remember that the stronger the relationship, the stronger the confrontation may be. If we have just begun a helper relationship, we must be careful not to move into confrontation prematurely. Before a relationship can usually survive confrontation, empathy and genuine concern must be established over a period of time. However, once a solid relationship has been established, offering an opportunity for people to see that "what they are saying is not what they are doing" can be a key that opens their awareness.

Helper confrontations can be passive, aggressive, or assertive. The assertive response is the one that most responsibly points out the discrepancy between people's words and their actions or apparent feelings.

Respond to each of the situations below by using a passive, an aggressive, and an assertive response:

Example

Friend:
"Things are going really well between Karen and me now. It does seem like she never has time to talk or do anything with me anymore, but we're really a lot closer now."

> **Helper** (Passive):
> *"I'm glad things are so good between you two."*

> **Helper** (Aggressive):
> *"Which one of us are you trying to fool?"*

> **Helper** (Assertive):
> *"You say that things are much better, but you actually sound depressed to me. It seems like your relationship with Karen is still a bit unsettled."*

1. Friend:
"Lately my parents have been getting along perfectly. Oh, sure, they still fight. As a matter of fact, they had a real blow-out last night! But, really, I'm feeling a lot better about them now."

Helper (Passive):

Helper (Aggressive):

Helper (Assertive):

2. Friend:
"I don't have a drinking problem! I never drink before lunch, and the only time I get drunk is on the weekend."

Helper (Passive):

Helper (Aggressive):

Helper (Assertive):

3. Friend:
"Well, my father said last night that he's going to start making my little brother help with the chores. I wonder how long it will last this time? Anyway, I guess I'm going to get some help, for a little while at least. It's nice to have that problem solved finally."

Helper (Passive):

Helper (Aggressive):

Helper (Assertive):

4. Friend:

"I know I deserved an A on that paper! I worked with Bob. He got an A! Sure, maybe he did some more research and stuff like that on his. But, really, I worked almost as hard as he did, and I got a lousy C!"

Helper (Passive):

Helper (Aggressive):

Helper (Assertive):

5. Friend:

"She's been spreading rumors about me again. She makes me so sick! Every time I see her I just give her the dirtiest look I can. I'll show her I'm above all her childish games. I'll just keep on ignoring her so she knows I couldn't care less!"

Helper (Passive):

Helper (Aggressive):

Helper (Assertive):

Now think of one area in your life in which you could benefit from confrontation, an area in which you could use to examine your behavior more closely. Write a response in which you passively allow yourself to continue the behavior, one in which you confront yourself aggressively, and one in which you confront yourself assertively.

Situation:

(Passive)

(Aggressive)

(Assertive)

Skills Chart

Make a check mark in one of the boxes next to a behavior each time the behavior is demonstrated:

I. Attending Skill

Sits facing the person	☐ ☐ ☐ ☐ ☐
Maintains good eye contact	☐ ☐ ☐ ☐ ☐
Maintains open, available posture	☐ ☐ ☐ ☐ ☐
Appears relaxed	☐ ☐ ☐ ☐ ☐
Gives encouragement, such as nodding head	☐ ☐ ☐ ☐ ☐

II. Empathy Skill

Reflects feelings, using different words	☐ ☐ ☐ ☐ ☐
Reflects content, using different words	☐ ☐ ☐ ☐ ☐

III. Clarifying/Questioning Skill

Uses clarifying questions or statements	☐ ☐ ☐ ☐ ☐
Asks open questions	☐ ☐ ☐ ☐ ☐
Asks closed questions	☐ ☐ ☐ ☐ ☐

IV. Assertiveness Skill

Uses "I" messages	☐ ☐ ☐ ☐ ☐
Uses "You" messages	☐ ☐ ☐ ☐ ☐

V. Confrontation Skill

Is nonconfrontive	☐ ☐ ☐ ☐ ☐
Uses aggressive confrontation	☐ ☐ ☐ ☐ ☐
Uses assertive confrontation	☐ ☐ ☐ ☐ ☐

Chapter 7

Problem-Solving Skill

The sixth, and last, skill of peer helping is that of problem-solving. Problem-solving is the last skill discussed as a reminder that all the other skills are necessary in building the foundation for problem-solving. When used effectively and in sequence, all the other skills lead naturally into problem-solving. People make changes in their lives when they feel important and worthwhile, understand their feelings, and take responsibility for creating the life they want to live.

The most important step in problem-solving is to let go of the belief that we are controlled by circumstances and to accept that we have choice and responsibility. Without achieving this attitude, there will be no effective solution found for any situation. Instead, no matter what other steps are taken, people end up sabotaging their own plan. They do this either out of a deep feeling that they deserve what is happening or because they are secretly getting something out of the situation.

Once the appropriate mental attitude is achieved, the process of problem-solving begins with the development of a plan of action. A plan requires us to focus thoroughly on a situation so that our solution is more likely to bring us the results we desire.

Problem-Solving Steps for Developing a Plan of Action

Identify the specifics of the problem. Become clear on the problem. Look at your feelings and responses within the situation. Consider the elements of the problem: who, what, where, when. Most of all, know how the problem situation is different from your ideal situation!

Brainstorm alternatives. Focus on those choices within your control. Look at what *you* can begin doing differently, not what you wish the world would do differently. Generate a list of alternatives that includes every response you could make, even those which seem impossible or unrealistic.

Consider the consequences of each alternative. Since everything we do and think (cause) has its consequence (effect), decide which cause and effect combination you want to experience. It sometimes helps to make a list of all the PROs and CONs of each alternative. Remember that how we choose to think and feel is always one of our alternatives. Strive for growth choices and avoid fear choices.

Make a contract. Verbally or in written form express your intention and plan of action. Include in your contract the specific steps to be taken, the obstacles which may need to be overcome, and a clear timeline of action. Share your plan of action with another person who is in a position to help you monitor your progress.

Use visualization. Visualize yourself as being successful beyond your greatest dreams in your chosen plan of action. See this as an already accomplished fact. Feel your success, see your reaction and that of others, and delight in the feeling.

Do it. All the planning in the world will get you no where if you are not willing to take action. Your choice is to live with the situation as it is or to take steps to create an environment of greater joy and satisfaction for yourself.

Evaluate the plan. Continue to adjust and develop, or even revise, the plan of action to keep pace with your perception of the situation. Problem-solving is not a static process. It is growth, which means it is a constantly developing process.

Personal Priorities

In making choices in our day to day decisions as well as in our major life decisions, we must be clear on what is most important to us. Below is a list of 15 personal priorities. Arrange them in order of their importance in YOUR life for YOUR happiness. Avoid the "shoulds" and "can'ts" and develop your list of "coulds." Put a "1" next to your highest priority, a "2" next to the second most important, and so on.

_____ CREATIVITY (expressing new ideas or talents)
_____ EXCITEMENT (high interest and stimulation)
_____ FUN (having the time of your life)
_____ INTEGRITY (honesty and honor)
_____ KNOWLEDGE (wisdom and awareness)
_____ LOVE (self, friends, family)
_____ MONEY (security and abundance)
_____ PERSONAL GROWTH (process of becoming)
_____ PHYSICAL DEVELOPMENT (healthy and attractive body)
_____ PURPOSE (meaning and contribution)
_____ POWER (ability to influence others)
_____ RECOGNITION (acknowledgment of others)
_____ SERENITY (acceptance and peace of mind)
_____ SERVICE (sharing personal skills and resources)
_____ SPIRITUALITY (connectedness to a higher power)

In establishing priorities, it is important to recognize that they are a part of our evolving growth, and they will be different at different times in our lives. Since each of the priorities above can be important to a well-balanced life, this list can be seen as a directory of the different characteristics that can be developed in a lifetime, rather than as a choice for or against.

No-Lose Problem-Solving:
Life Doesn't Have to be a
No-Win or Win-Lose Proposition

Too many of life's situations are approached with an "I win, you lose" attitude. In personal relationships, the problem with being a winner is then there must be a loser, who may want to be the winner next time. This sets up a destructive and totally unnecessary condition in a relationship. For example, let's say you and I are trying to decide where we will go for dinner. I want Mexican food, and you want Italian food. I absolutely refuse to have Italian food and insist on having Mexican food. So, you agree, however reluctantly or resentfully, to have Mexican food. This is called a WIN-LOSE SOLUTION and is an example of aggressive/passive problem-solving.

A second way that people approach a disagreement is to make sure that both people loose. The message here seems to be that as long as I can't have what I want, then I'll see that you don't get what you want either. For example, this time when I refuse to have Italian food, you also refuse to have Mexican food. Neither one of us is willing to have what the other one wants, so we end up having a hamburger at a fast food restaurant we both hate. This is called a NO-WIN SOLUTION and is an example of aggressive/aggressive problem-solving.

However, NO-WIN SOLUTIONS can also take the form of passive/passive problem-solving. Have you ever watched a couple who are trying to decide where to go for dinner, and he says, "I don't know. Where do you want to go?" And she says, "I don't know. Where do you want to go?" This, too, is NO-WIN problem-solving.

The most caring and creative way to approach a disagreement is to look for a solution which satisfies both people equally. Because they are both winners, there are no losers. Sometimes the solution involves a compromise. Other times, it involves an approach of imagination and insight in which both people feel they have gained. For example, when I want Mexican food and you want Italian food, we might have Italian food this time and Mexican food next time. Or, we might find a fun little restaurant bazaar where they serve several kinds of food in the same location. Or, we could remind ourselves that we have been meaning to experiment more, and we could decide to try that great looking new Chinese restaurant. These are called NO-LOSE SOLUTIONS and are examples of assertive/assertive problem-solving.

Here are some steps to follow in developing NO-LOSE SOLUTIONS in your own life:

Decide that you want a NO-LOSE relationship. Before it makes any sense to learn the steps in NO-LOSE problem-solving, you must first have decided that you want a relationship based on equality of needs, feelings, and wants. This is the most important of all the steps because without this desire, these are just so many words.

Understand the disagreement. Make sure you each understand what the other person is feeling and thinking about the situation. Generally, when you are able to understand what another person is experiencing, the solution to the disagreement begins to develop naturally.

Clarify your understanding. If you have questions or you begin to see connections between this situation and others that have occurred, spend some time discussing these ideas. This is how a disagreement, which seems like the worst thing that could happen, can lead to a stronger connection between two people, becoming the best thing that could happen!

Brainstorm solutions. Have some fun with this! Laughter is healing and can get us over some of the roughest places in our lives. However, laughter is a double-edged sword, so make sure you always laugh *at* yourself, but *with* others. Let your imaginations go in developing this list of possible solutions. Also, use this as an opportunity to demonstrate your caring and appreciation for the other person through the solutions you suggest.

Pick one. No decision is forever. Choose the one which seems to satisfy the needs of both people best at this time. Look at PROs and CONs, if that seems helpful. Realize, too, that new understanding and commitment is the greatest gain that has been made in this process. Decide to reevaluate this decision periodically and to look at adjustments which might be made. Relationships are constantly evolving, so decisions affecting them need to evolve also.

Goals:
Because If You Don't Know Where You Are Going, You Will Undoubtedly End Up Somewhere Else

Select a goal. Know what you want. So often, we don't get what we want, because we haven't been able to decide what that is. Choose something you would like to change, nave, or improve.

Picture your goal. What we can conceive and believe, we can achieve. Create a mental picture of what you want, putting yourself in the picture. Let your imagination go and picture the absolutely ideal situation for you. Picture it as if it already exists and go into great detail seeing sights, smelling smells, and feeling how it feels to experience your goal.

Write down your goal. Write a description of your ideal situation including all of the details. Or, draw a picture of yourself in your ideal situation. Read it or look at it often, making changes if you want. Think about your goal at night before you go to sleep and in the morning when you wake up.

Select sub-goals. Especially if your goal is a long-term goal, look at the short-term goals which will help you to accomplish your major goal. Decide what you need to do today, next week, next month, next year, and so on. Choose short-term goals that you can accomplish. Use them to signal your progress toward your major goal and to develop your sense of achievement. If you fail to accomplish some of your short-term goals, do not become discouraged or criticize yourself. Instead, choose new short-term goals or renew your dedication to your original ones.

Limit yourself. Don't try to do too much at one time. You'll find that you are most effective if you focus on one major goal at a time. Once you are experiencing progress toward your major goal, you can move on to new areas of goal setting. If you find yourself feeling discouraged or overwhelmed, simplify your goal. Goals are intended to make you feel good about yourself and to point you in the direction you want to go. Make sure you are focusing on goals that you desire enough that you are willing to work to accomplish them.

Reward yourself. As you see progress toward your goal or when you achieve a goal, acknowledge yourself with a pat on the back or by doing something nice for yourself. As the good friend we are learning to be to ourselves, it's nice to have someone notice!

Skills Chart

Make a check mark in one of the boxes next to a behavior each time the behavior is demonstrated:

I. Attending Skill

Sits facing the person   ☐ ☐ ☐ ☐ ☐
Maintains good eye contact   ☐ ☐ ☐ ☐ ☐
Maintains open, available posture   ☐ ☐ ☐ ☐ ☐
Appears relaxed   ☐ ☐ ☐ ☐ ☐
Gives encouragement, such as nodding   ☐ ☐ ☐ ☐ ☐
head

II. Empathy Skill

Reflects feelings, using different words   ☐ ☐ ☐ ☐ ☐
Reflects content, using different words   ☐ ☐ ☐ ☐ ☐

III. Clarifying/Questioning Skill

Uses clarifying questions or statements   ☐ ☐ ☐ ☐ ☐
Asks open questions   ☐ ☐ ☐ ☐ ☐
Asks closed questions   ☐ ☐ ☐ ☐ ☐

IV. Assertiveness Skill

Uses "I" messages   ☐ ☐ ☐ ☐ ☐
Uses "You" messages   ☐ ☐ ☐ ☐ ☐

V. Confrontation Skill

Is nonconfrontive   ☐ ☐ ☐ ☐ ☐
Uses aggressive confrontation   ☐ ☐ ☐ ☐ ☐
Uses assertive confrontation   ☐ ☐ ☐ ☐ ☐

VI. Problem-Solving Skill

Facilitates problem identification   ☐ ☐ ☐ ☐ ☐
Facilitates brainstorming of alternatives   ☐ ☐ ☐ ☐ ☐
Facilitates evaluation of alternatives/
consequences   ☐ ☐ ☐ ☐ ☐
Facilitates plan of action or goal   ☐ ☐ ☐ ☐ ☐
development

Peer Helping Skills Exam

For each skill, tell what you have learned about the purpose and benefits of the skill, the types of situations in which it is particularly helpful, and any personal observations or insights you have to offer:

1. Attending Skill

2. Empathy Skill

3. Clarifying/Questioning Skill

4. Assertiveness Skill

5. Confrontation Skill

6. Problem-Solving Skill

Unit III
Topic Development

Chapter 8
Suicide Prevention and Intervention

It is estimated that approximately 1000 teens attempt suicide every day, and their friends and classmates are likely to be in the best position to stop them. Most depressed teenagers will confide in their peers before they will talk with an adult. Peer counselors who are known to be caring, understanding people are especially likely to be among those peers whom others turn to for help. Learning to recognize the warning signs and to understand what is being communicated may allow you to be the friend someone needs.

Suicide: Myths or Facts?

T   F   1. Suicide is against the law in this state.

T   F   2. A person usually commits suicide without warning.

T   F   3. Most suicide attempts occur late at night and away from home.

T   F   4. It is dangerous to talk about suicide with a depressed person.

T   F   5. Use of alcohol and other drugs can increase the risk of suicide.

T   F   6. Suicidal people want to die, and they will find a way to succeed eventually.

T   F   7. More females than males commit suicide.

T   F   8. People who talk about suicide rarely do it.

T   F   9. Depressed people are the greatest suicidal risks.

T   F 10. Suicidal people are mentally ill.

T   F 11. Once people become suicidal, they will be suicidal forever.

T   F 12. Suicide occurs most often among the poor.

T   F 13. Suicidal people rarely seek medical attention.

T   F 14. If people make an unsuccessful suicide attempt, they probably won't ever make another attempt.

T   F 15. Suicide rates are increasing among the young.

Suicide: The Facts

1. Suicide is not against the law in most states. This can sometimes severely limit the ability of law enforcement and social agencies to intervene.

2. Although suicide is sometimes impulsive, it is usually planned well in advance and then hinted at or actually communicated to others.

3. Most suicide attempts take place in the home, often in the late afternoon or early evening, when friends and family are mostly likely to be able to intervene.

4. Allowing people to talk about their suicidal thoughts provides relief and a sense of being understood and accepted. This is a strong deterrent to suicidal behavior because it encourages the ventilation of repressed feelings and a frank discussion of the problem.

5. Use of alcohol and other drugs vastly reduces the fear of death. Over 50 percent of adolescents who committed suicide had been using alcohol or other drugs.

6. Suicidal people are ambivalent about life. They don't actually want to die, but they're also not sure they want to live. They are actually more anti-life than they are pro-death. Adolescents in particular really want to be rescued but often don't know who or how to ask for help. They will sometimes just gamble with death, leaving it to others to save them.

7. Although females attempt suicide three times as often as males, males actually kill themselves four times as often as females.

8. Most people who kill themselves have hinted at suicide or have actually told someone they were going to kill themselves.

9. Depression is such a draining emotion that it often im-
   mobilizes people. The greatest danger comes during
   the three months after people begin to recover from a
   deep depression. This is when they will have the
   energy to actually carry out a plan.

10. "Normal" people kill themselves every day. Although
    a small percentage of suicidal people are mentally ill,
    most suicidal people are just severely depressed and
    feeling hopeless. They simply haven't been able to find
    another way to stop the pain.

11. Most people are suicidal only for a limited period of
    time. If they are given support and assistance, most of
    them go on to lead normal lives and never again ex-
    perience a suicidal crisis.

12. Suicidal behavior is not limited to any particular eco-
    nomic status. It occurs proportionately among all
    levels of society.

13. It is estimated that over 50 percent of suicidal people
    had visited a physician for nonspecific medical atten-
    tion within three to six months of killing themselves.

14. Four out of five people who succeed in killing them-
    selves have already made at least one previous at-
    tempt. It is estimated that about half of those who try
    once will try again.

15. Suicide is now the second leading cause of death, after
    accidents, for youth between the ages of 15 and 24
    years. The suicide rate for this age group has been in-
    creasing ten times faster than any other age group and
    has more than doubled in the last 20 years.

Suicide: The Ultimate Tragedy

About 6,000 teenagers kill themselves every year, making suicide the second leading cause of death, after accidents, among 15-24 year olds. For every suicide attempt that succeeds, there are an estimated 50 that do not! While more females than males attempt suicide, males are more often successful because they tend to choose more lethal methods.

It is believed that most people think about suicide at some time in their lives. Having such thoughts is considered normal. However, why do so many young people today actually decide to act upon their suicidal thoughts? We must remember that adolescence is a time of change, starting with biological change. This causes new stress and uncertainty, resulting in new feelings of self-consciousness and inadequacy. Adolescence is born out of loss—the loss of childhood. Although this has always been the case, today new losses have been added to the old ones.

Because many of our cultural and moral ideas have changed, young people today find themselves struggling with new freedoms, often without any new understanding. This causes them to experience new levels of confusion. Adults today are also frequently dealing with the same feelings of confusion and are searching for more meaningful life styles. Because of this, young people today regularly deal with new homes, new schools, new friends, and new parents. Although these experiences can bring new strength to a young person who feels loved and cherished, adolescents often find themselves "in the way" and cast aside in their parents' search for a new life. Many adolescents experience a new and profound loneliness, that of *not belonging* to anyone. If this feeling is compounded by any new loss, the result is often devastating.

Adolescents today also experience more pressure. The American dream of living the "good life" seems to have led to an unhealthy and often crippling pressure to get into the "best" college and to choose the "right" career. Success is defined as monetary gain, often at the expense of personal growth or contribution to mankind. In addition, there is increased social pressure for adolescents today. The average age that teenagers become sexually active and begin using alcohol and other drugs is lower than ever before. Influenced by the messages they see and hear on television and in the movies, many adolescents experiment in these areas without being ready to handle themselves.

When all of the pressures to do the right things and to look and act just right are compounded by the difficulty many adults have in managing their lives, many troubled teenagers begin to see death as an attractive alternative. Yet adults often respond to young people who talk about the pressures they are experiencing by saying, "But these are the best times of your life!" This only succeeds in making young people think, "Do you mean it gets *worse*?" Suicide becomes a way to find peace and to escape from conflicts and pressures which feel overwhelming.

Adolescents frequently lack the perspective to see that their problems will end. They forget, or haven't experienced, that the dark times pass, problems get solved, and life feels good again. The media has added to this problem in another way also. Many young people have grown up watching life's problems reduced to a 30-60 minute formula on television. Unfortunately, this has led many adolescents to believe that there should always be an immediate solution to every problem. When this is not their actual experience, many young people simply are not equipped to work their way through a difficult situation. Again, death becomes an attractive alternative.

Young people who are feeling this deeply distressed will give warning signs which can alert someone that they may be considering suicide. Each individual warning sign is indicative of trouble and needs to be dealt with by a straightforward expression of concern. If several of these warning signs are occurring simultaneously, immediate intervention must occur. The warning signs of impending suicide include, but are not limited to:

1. talking or hinting about committing suicide, including having made a previous suicide gesture or attempt;

2. personality changes, such as a normally aggressive person suddenly becoming passive or a passive person suddenly becoming aggressive;

3. sudden changes in eating or sleeping patterns, such as overeating, loss of appetite, inability to sleep, or sleeping all the time;

4. a dramatic drop in school performance and/or a sudden disinterest in personal appearance;

5. themes of suicide or death in stories, poems, or other works of art;

6. withdrawal from family and friends;

7. listening to the same sad songs over and over or listening to music which causes a frenzy of destructive thoughts;

8. a sudden unexplained happy mood after a period of deep depression;

9. making a will or giving away prized possessions, especially those which were never shared before; and

10. purchasing a gun, knife, rope, or other type of weapon, including heavy use of alcohol or other drugs.

What should you do if someone you know seems to fit this description? First, always take any mention of suicide seriously no matter how often you have heard it from that person. One of the most dangerous and popularly accepted myths is that people who talk about suicide never do it. WRONG! More than 75 percent of all suicide victims have talked about it beforehand. Don't fall into the trap of thinking that such talk is *just* for attention. Of course it is for attention. More importantly, it is a cry for help! People will not usually resort to this way of asking for help when they know a more effective way to do it.

Openly and gently express your concern by describing the person's behavior. Offer your observations but avoid analyzing the behavior. The "why's" of what people do or feel can only come from them. Bring up the subject of suicide by asking if they have been thinking about it. Don't be afraid that by talking about suicide you will be giving the person ideas. This is just another popular myth, born of the desire not to have to deal with the problem.

A person who is seriously considering suicide *already has the idea!* Someone in this much pain will be grateful for your sensitivity and concern and will be relieved at the opportunity to talk about it. People who aren't thinking of suicide won't begin thinking about it just because you bring up the topic. However, they will certainly have a new perspective on their behavior, and they will undoubtedly be touched that you cared enough to deal with a difficult subject.

Encourage the person to talk about what has been happening. Show you care by listening intently with a great deal of acceptance and understanding. The more you can help people to express and understand their pain and fears, the more they will move away from the idea of suicide.

However, this is not enough to insure that a person will remain safe. You are an important part of the support system for a person who is suicidal, but you must never take the responsibility for such a situation! This is a secret which simply cannot be kept, and it is a secret which the person unconsciously doesn't want kept! Sometimes we have to be willing to risk a friendship in order to help a friend.

Anyone who has been in a school where there has been a student suicide comes to understand the absolute necessity for involving adults who can help. However, it is a sad fact that most young people who have *not* been in such a situation will be resistant to this idea. If you ever ask yourself the question, "Should I tell someone?" remember that the answer is always YES! Know the system of referral within your program and be willing to use it! *Don't ever be the last person someone talked to about suicide.*

The person's family must be notified, and this notification is best made by one of the professionals in your school or community. It is sometimes hard for young people to accept that the family will be notified because they often feel that the family is a big part of the problem! However, people usually handle true emergencies better than they handle the day to day hassles of living. Parents are no exception. Most parents simply don't realize how bad it has become for their son or daughter, and they both deserve and *must* be given the chance to help.

It helps to remember that most people really don't want to die. They just want the pain to stop. You can be an important part of helping a friend choose life.

Techniques of Assessment and Intervention

Assessment:

"HNDL" Assessment Technique

H : How HANDY or available is the method?
N : How NEAR is help?
D : How DETAILED or specific is the method?
L : How LETHAL is the method?

Questions to ask the potentially suicidal person:

- ☐ Has it been so bad lately that you have been thinking about suicide?
- ☐ How long have you been thinking about suicide?
- ☐ How often do you think about suicide?
- ☐ Have you decided how you would do it?
- ☐ Have you decided when you would do it?
- ☐ What has kept you from doing it so far?
- ☐ Why now?
- ☐ Have you ever tried to kill yourself before?

NOTE: If people have been drinking or using other substances, their responses cannot be considered reliable.

Intervention:

1. Establish a relationship by listening.
2. Encourage the person to express feelings.
3. Accept what is said without shock.
4. Identify problems, without dwelling on them excessively.
5. Identify positive alternatives.
6. Avoid stressing the shock and pain of family and friends as this is sometimes the motive.
7. Express the person's loss of life as being a personal loss for you, when you can do this genuinely.
8. Learn what is meaningful to the person and offer hope, being careful not to offer what you can't deliver.
9. Contract.
10. Make a referral to a counselor or crisis intervention program. If necessary, stay with the person until help arrives.

No-Suicide Contract

I, _____ , promise that I will not kill or hurt myself, accidentally or on purpose, from now until _____, when I agree to talk to my counselor, _____.

I agree to give everything I would use to kill or hurt myself, including _____

_____ to _____.

I also agree that if I start thinking about killing or hurting myself, I will talk to:

my counselor at _____, or

my friend _____ at _____, or

the crisis intervention program at _____.

Signed: _____

Witnessed: _____

Dated: _____

Levels of Suicidal Risk

Level I Risk

Some indicators of developing trouble:

A. Mild depression
B. Unusual aggressive or passive behaviors
C. Alcohol or substance abuse
D. Changes in eating or sleeping habits
E. Drop in school performance and/or unusual lack of interest in personal appearance
F. Family strife or impending divorce
G. Other recent loss or crisis

Characteristics:
These people are frequently communicating double messages, saying they are not having suicidal thoughts while their behavior suggests otherwise. They have no clear plan, no definite time frame, and no readily available method *as yet*. However, they are depressed and focused on death.

Example: people who write morbid poems or stories about death or who jokingly talk about suicide.

Intervention:
Contract
Referral to a counselor
Parental notification
Follow up

Level II Risk

Some indicators of developing risk:

A. Chronic depression
B. Abrupt changes in personality or sudden mood swings
C. Impulsive or extreme risk-taking behavior
D. Inability to concentrate
E. Withdrawal from friends and family
F. Divorce, change in family status, or a recent move to a new school

Characteristics:

These people are still ambivalent about suicide, but they are at the stage of having at least a vague plan or of having a plan that is not highly lethal. They will usually not yet have set a definite time or conceived of a readily available and highly lethal method. However, they are now beginning to *try out* the idea of suicide.

Example: people who say there is aspirin in the medicine cabinet, and they just might take them the next time things get really bad.

Intervention:

Contract
Referral to a counselor
Parental notification
Professional assessment and assistance
Follow up

Level III Risk

Some indicators of severe risk:

A. Acute depression
B. Talk of helplessness, hopelessness, haplessness
C. Talk of being dead
D. Making a will or giving away possessions
E. Suicidal gestures
F. Loss of an important person or loss of status
G. Failure to achieve long sought goal
H. Trouble with authorities
I. Purchasing a weapon
J. Previous suicide attempt

Characteristics:
These people will have made a definite plan or have set a definite time. They have a readily available and highly lethal method. They will often begin subtly saying good-bye to people, perhaps by visiting someone they have not seen for awhile.

Example: people who keep a gun and ammunition under the bed and who decide that this Saturday when the family is out of town, that they are going to use it.

Intervention:
Restrain if necessary and possible, but *NEVER* try to take a weapon away forcibly
Call police and/or crisis intervention program
Referral to a counselor
Parental notification
Professional assessment and assistance
Follow up

It is important to realize that people do not necessarily work through the levels of suicidal risk in order! It is possible for the first indication of trouble to show itself in Level III characteristics!! It is also possible for a person to go from Level I to Level III in a *very* short period of time if enough additional things go wrong!!!

Your job is never to take responsibility for other people, but to recognize when they need help, let them know you care, and get them to the help they need.

Chapter 9

Alcoholism

It is possible to understand most forms of chemical dependency by understanding the progression of the disease of alcoholism. Also, alcohol is the most commonly abused of all drugs, and alcoholism is the number one health problem in our country today. It is now estimated that 1 in 10 people are alcoholic and 1 in 4 children live in alcoholic homes. Alcoholism is a problem which affects millions of people, including some of your friends or acquaintances and perhaps your family or yourself.

Alcoholism is a primary, chronic, progressive, potentially fatal disease.

- It is a *primary* disease because it *is* the problem and is not just a symptom of a problem. By the time problem drinking has reached the stage of alcoholism, it has taken on the properties and dynamics of a disease. Attempts to treat alcoholism simply by treating underlying problems have been notably unsuccessful.

- It is a *chronic* disease because, so far as can be determined, no one who has become alcoholic has ever ceased to be alcoholic. Alcoholism can be treated, but it can never be cured. A recovering alcoholic can never safely use alcohol again.

- It is a *progressive* disease because there are stages in the development of alcoholism. If left untreated, it will get worse. Also, if alcoholics quit drinking for several years and then start again, within a few weeks they will be drinking as much as if they had never stopped.

- It is a *potentially fatal* disease. People drink themselves to death through an overdose (called alcohol poisoning), or by degeneration of organs such as the liver, kidneys, pancreas, heart, and brain, or by being killed in a car accident while driving under the influence. Without treatment, alcoholism invariably leads to premature death.

There appears to be a genetic predisposition toward the development of alcoholism. More than half of all alcoholics have an alcoholic parent. If people have two alcoholic parents, they have a 50 percent chance of becoming alcoholic. An alcoholic's body functions differently from a non-alcoholic's by metabolizing alcohol differently. It is not necessarily when or how much people drink, but *what happens* when they drink, that indicates a problem.

The progressive steps to alcoholism, given by Alcoholics Anonymous, are described below:

1. **You have begun to drink.**
   You find that alcohol serves a friendly social purpose. You have a few beers or some wine now and then. Once in a while you have too much, but in the morning you can't stand the thought of alcohol. After the hangover, you are fine. The odds are that most people will never go past this step. However, others move imperceptibly to the next step.

2. **You experience a growing preoccupation with drinking.** You now find yourself anticipating your periods of drinking. You look forward to the next "kegger," or you use playing softball or going on a camping trip as an excuse to do a lot of heavy drinking. You find that if there won't be drinking at an activity, you aren't interested in going. You experience a growing tolerance, drinking everyone else "under the table." You also begin to experience a growing need for alcohol in times of stress.

3. You start having "blackouts."

You are getting drunk with some regularity now. You are one of a crowd that likes to drink quite a bit, particularly on the weekends. Even so, you still feel you can stop any time you want. Then one night you put away your usual amount, and the next day you can't remember how you got home or anything else after a certain time. A period of life simply is gone from your memory, but you did not "pass out." You had a "blackout." A "blackout" is an alcohol-induced amnesia, often involving several hours. During this time, people are totally conscious and behaving in a normal way. However, it is a period of time which they are later unable to remember. A "blackout" is caused by an electrical imbalance in the brain brought about by the use of a chemical, and it is a warning sign of developing alcoholism.

4. You find alcohol means more to you than to others.

About the time you start having "blackouts," you change from sipping drinks to gulping them. You want that "kick" more than you used to. You also start sneaking drinks. During a party, you take one or two extras when no one is looking, or you have a couple before the party to be sure you will enjoy yourself. At this point, you can still stop if you recognize what is happening. If not, your chances of becoming an alcoholic are very high.

_____DANGER LINE_____

5. You are consistently drinking more than you intend.

You find almost every time you take a drink, you drink more than you had planned. You go to a party firmly resolved to have just two drinks, and you wind up drunk without knowing how it happened. You can no longer control the amount you drink on a given occasion.

6. **You start excusing yourself for drinking.**

   You have begun making excuses for your loss of control. In spite of appearances, you tell yourself you really *can* handle alcohol. But you've had a bad day, or it's your best friend's birthday, or you had another fight with your parents, boss, teachers, girlfriend, boyfriend, and so forth. There is always a reason why you drink too much. The fact is you now feel guilty about your drinking. You have begun to lie to yourself and other people.

7. **You start taking "eye-openers."**

   You begin taking a drink the first thing in the morning to get yourself started. You take it not for pleasure but as a kind of medicine. You tell yourself you *need* it. You are depressed and a little shaky from the heavy drinking of the night before. The drink eases your conscience. It lifts your ego. It also helps strengthen the process of self-deceit which is making you more and more dependent on alcohol.

8. **You begin to drink alone.**

   Not long after you start drinking in the morning, you find that you really prefer drinking alone. You prefer not to share the pleasure alcohol gives you. You drink only to escape into the private, distorted world of your imagination—a world where you tell off your boss or parents, amaze your friends with your brilliance, or become a great poet or financial whiz. What you cannot see now is that drinking has become a flight from reality into fantasy.

9. **You become antisocial when you drink.**

   Solitary drinking is already antisocial. However, with some people there is a further step—a violent one. You pick fights with strangers for no good reason. You smash things. You pull practical jokes in which someone could be hurt. Or, you become extremely self-conscious and wary of people, afraid they are staring at you and whispering about you. All this is a sign that drinking has distorted your judgment. Your remedy for that is more alcohol.

_____DANGER LINE_____

10. You start going on benders.
The acute stage of your compulsive drinking begins now. You are a true alcoholic. This stage usually comes one to three years after you have begun drinking in the morning. A bender is a period of time during which you drink blindly, helplessly, with just one goal: to get drunk. You disregard family, friends, job—even food and shelter. To get more alcohol you will lie, pawn your best possessions, and steal. Later, you may try to go "on the wagon" for awhile. This works if you stay "on the wagon" for life. But you only plan to quit drinking for a short period, and then you go back to your former ways. You tell yourself these periods of sobriety give you a chance to recuperate, but you really do it to prove to yourself, and to others, that you can still quit. But you can't quit, because you do not really intend to quit.

11. You experience repeated harmful consequences from drinking. It is all beginning to crash in on you now. You are experiencing trouble in your family. You also are running into legal trouble with traffic violations or charges of being drunk and disorderly. You have lost most of your friends and your associations within the community. You have been passed over for several promotions at work, and now your job is on the line.

12. You know deep remorse and resentment.
You have sober moments when you feel deep remorse. However, working against this is the deep-seated conviction that you have good reasons for drinking, but nobody tried to understand. When your excuses prove

too weak, you begin resenting others. You start having fits of anger over little things, or nothing at all. A friend forgets to call, someone leaves a bike in the driveway, you recall a chance remark someone made last week, and you become furious.

13. You feel deep, nameless anxiety.
The steps to emotional and spiritual bankruptcy are coming faster and closer together. You begin to feel a vague but ever present fear. You show it to the world by your trembling hands, vacant stares, and jittery nerves. People call it "the shakes." It is as much an expression of your fear as it is a physical reaction.

14. You realize your drinking has beat you.
The day comes when you admit to yourself that you can't handle alcohol. Perhaps you have awakened to find yourself in the hospital or in jail. You finally accept that you are powerless over alcohol, and your life has become unmanageable.

15. You get help or you go under.
Now you face the ultimate choice: get help or give up. You have thrown away love, respect, and security. Your only comfort, alcohol, has proved false. Although you are seriously ill, you can recover. It will take your strength and that of many others, plus time and a certain knowledge that you can never touch alcohol again. The alternative is to stay where you are until you die. Hope lies in facing the facts and asking for help *now*, while there is still time.

The disease of alcoholism is also a family disease, called codependency. It becomes a primary coping disease within each family member. In the chemically dependent family, the members adapt to the behavior of the *Dependent* in a way which causes them the least amount of personal stress. Unfortunately, this generally means that they compulsively repress their feelings, becoming locked into a set of rigid survival behaviors which are designed only to build a defense against the pain.

Codependency is characterized by preoccupation with feelings of being responsible for the behavior and welfare of another person. This sets up a pattern of reacting to others in ways that become self-defeating and destructive. The longer people use a particular role to cope, the more rigidly fixed it becomes. They eventually become addicted to their role, identifying themselves *as the role.*

In her extraordinary book, *Another Chance: Hope and Health for the Alcoholic Family,* Sharon Wegscheider identifies the survival roles that develop within the alcoholic family. The members of the family find, or are given, these survival roles as their way of dealing with the pain.

The first survival role is that of the *Chief Enabler,* who is usually the parent or spouse. However, it is important to note that in the alcoholic family, all of the family members do their part to protect the Dependent, thereby participating in the process of enabling. The Chief Enabler is the person who is closest to the Dependent and is the one who is relied upon most heavily. As the Dependent loses more and more control, the Chief Enabler becomes more and more responsible, making decisions to compensate for the Dependent's loss of power. The Chief Enabler will also be the one to provide the excuses and to cover up for the Dependent with the boss, other family members, neighbors, or anyone else. Chief Enablers do not mean to make matters worse, but they do by providing a cushion between the Dependents and the consequences of their actions. This only succeeds in delaying the day of reckoning. One of the most difficult things for Chief Enablers to recognize is that they have become a part of the problem. The defenses the Chief Enabler chooses are those of super-responsibility, manipulation, and self-pity to cover up feelings of fear, guilt, and especially anger. The role of the Chief Enabler is to provide responsibility for the family.

The *Hero* is usually the oldest child. This person senses some of what is happening in the family and feels responsible for all the pain. The Hero learns early that the best way to stay out of trouble is to be very, very good. The Hero works hard to make things better by providing success for the family. The motivation for the Hero's achievements is to make up for the imbalances and pain of the family rather than to satisfy personal desires. However, because the disease of chemical dependency is a progressive one, the Hero constantly feels inadequate and deals with this by trying all the harder. Heroes are frequently very difficult to intervene with because they are so competent and successful. They will often respond to statements of concern with great surprise. After all, look how successful they are. What could be wrong? The defenses the Hero chooses are those of being all-together, successful, and responsible to cover up feelings of confusion, inadequacy, and anger. The role of the Hero is to provide self-worth for the family.

The *Scapegoat* is the one in the family who gets negative attention by running away, getting pregnant, defying authority, or by getting heavily into alcohol or other drugs. Scapegoats realize that in their family people are not accepted for who they are but for how they perform. However, no matter how hard Scapegoats try, they can never gain the acceptance and approval given to the Hero. Eventually they give up trying to prove themselves worthy. While the Hero is being "good" and responsible, the Scapegoat becomes "bad" and irresponsible. Scapegoats usually withdraw from their family and find feelings of acceptance somewhere else, often with others who are also dealing with deep feelings of frustration and rejection. The defenses the Scapegoat chooses are those of rebelliousness, sullenness, and stubbornness to cover up feelings of anger, rejection, and pain. The role of the Scapegoat is to provide distraction for the family.

Like the Scapegoat, the *Lost Child* feels like an outsider. However, rather than resorting to the attention getting behaviors of the Scapegoat, this child adapts by "getting lost." The Lost Child becomes a loner, having learned that it is safest not to get too close to anyone. These children spend most of their time staying quietly busy and away from the chaos in the family, where they are generally overlooked anyway. The Lost Child rarely gets much attention of any kind, positive or negative. The Lost Child's deep lack of self-worth is the result of all the years of being ignored. Because the Lost Child is "just there," this is one child the family does not have to worry about. The defenses the Lost Child chooses are independence and distance to cover up feelings of pain, loneliness, worthlessness, but little or no anger. The role of the Lost Child is to provide welcome relief for the family.

The *Mascot* tends to be the youngest child in the family. Mascots bring fun and humor to their family in order to lighten the atmosphere. They are often clever and charming, but they can also be hyperactive and annoying. The natural tendency of any family to protect the youngest is intensified in this family with all its pain and secrets. As a result, family members often withhold information or deliberately give misleading information to the Mascot. Because of this, Mascots suffer great confusion and anxiety. Their senses say that something is terribly wrong in the family, but everyone denies or ignores any and all questions. What Mascots do know is that while entertaining or distracting the family, they can control the family scene for as long as they can hold the floor. This provides a sense of security for a short time. The defenses the Mascot chooses are clowning, being super-cute, and doing anything for a laugh or for attention to cover up feelings of fear, insecurity, and confusion. The role of the Mascot is to provide fun and humor, or distraction, for the family.

The family members becomes locked into these survival roles, almost always without realizing it. Because the survival roles work to offer some protection from the growing pain and fear, the family members become compulsive in their behaviors. Without intervention, they will take these behaviors into every relationship and situation in their lives. The defense system of repressed feelings and survival roles has now become a primary problem for each family member.

Both chemical dependency and codependency are diseases of denial, delusion, and compulsion. As the dependency and the resultant codependency progress, denial, delusion, and compulsion become a part of every family member's reaction so that none of them recognize what is happening. Because chemical dependency affects the whole person and the whole family, effective treatment must also be designed for the whole person and the whole family.

Until recently, it was generally accepted that the Dependent had to "hit bottom" and voluntarily seek help before anything could be done. While this is accurate, by waiting until the crisis finally came, it was often too late to salvage much of a life. Now through a process called "Intervention," it is possible for those who care about the Dependent to *create a crisis*. This has the same effect for the Dependent as "hitting bottom," but without having to wait until everything has been lost. Alcoholics Anonymous, or AA, refers to this as hitting a "high bottom." While the decision to intervene is almost always a frightening and difficult one for the family, support and encouragement during the process can be found with groups such as Al-Anon and Alateen.

An Intervention should be done *only* under the direction of a professional. It combines the significant people in the Dependent's life together in a presentation to the Dependent. Those included in the Intervention will usually be the spouse, children, other family members, employer, best friend, and so on. This presentation is actually a script written by each person stating specific examples of times when the Dependent's behavior caused pain, fear, embarrassment, danger, or other problems. The scripts will include the exact time, setting, and all details of each episode. The effectiveness of this lies in the impact of heaping fact upon fact with little room for denial by the Dependent, *all offered in an atmosphere of love and deep concern*. Part of the planning for an Intervention also involves decisions about what treatment or course of action the Dependent will be asked to take. When an Intervention has been thoroughly planned and everyone involved has been thoroughly prepared, most Dependents will agree to seek treatment as a result.

Residential treatment for the Dependent will consist of detoxification care and individual and group counseling. Primary care for the family members will consist of individual and group counseling in order to break through their own denial, delusion, and compulsive behaviors. Without this work by the family members, the Dependent simply returns to the old family system with all the old behaviors, and the odds of relapse will be extraordinarily high.

By the time the Dependent leaves the treatment center, only a very small part of the necessary work within the family will have been accomplished. During After Care, the family members will begin their work together as a family. This is a time to deal with leftover problems and also with the new problems which occur as family members develop new behaviors and ways of communicating. In addition to working together as a family, many families also choose to participate in multi-family groups.

With the completion of After Care, the formal period of treatment ends for the recovering alcoholic and for the recovering family members. Recovery becomes a time for reaching out further in search of increased support and growth. Opportunities for this can be found with fellowships such as AA, Al-Anon, and Alateen, community support groups, workshops and seminars, clubs, and social activities. Recovery becomes a way of living that is based upon staying healthy rather than getting healthy.

But He (or She) Doesn't *Look* Like an Alcoholic

When you say "alcoholic" to most people, they picture a skid row bum. However, nothing could be further from the truth. An alcoholic also can be what is called a "functional alcoholic":

Functional alcoholics can be mothers, fathers, teachers, ministers, psychiatrists, truck drivers, lawyers, pilots, surgeons, neighbors, students, friends, or anyone else.

Functional alcoholics do *not* necessarily ever look or act drunk, miss a lot of work, drink in the morning or every weekend, get verbally or physically abusive, or have blackouts.

Functional alcoholics *do* have sleeping problems, sexual problems, family and relationship problems, problems of self-esteem, mood swings, explosions of anger, health problems, spiritual problems, or financial and legal problems.

Functional alcoholics *may* miss work—especially on Mondays—because of an upset stomach, bad back, sinus headache, allergies, ulcers and so on. They may want a drink as soon as they get home, need a drink before talking about anything unpleasant, make promises that aren't kept, brag about not drinking for a few days, weeks, or months, drink the first couple of drinks quickly, be uncomfortable where no alcohol is served, or not be able to remember conversations that occurred while they were drinking.

Functional alcoholics may have convinced the family members that *they are why* the functional alcoholic is irritable, gets sarcastic, likes to be alone, skips meals, has such wide mood swings, gets depressed, is forgetful, has money troubles, procrastinates, or isn't interested in doing things around the house or with the family.

Alcoholism Always Gives Warning Signs But Sometimes No One Listens

1. Have you ever rationalized your drinking?

2. Have you ever been embarrassed by your drinking?

3. Do you think that the best part of the party is the drinking?

4. Do you have to drink a lot to feel good?

5. Do you drink as a way to deal with problems or stresses?

6. Have you ever had a loss of memory as a result of drinking?

7. Have you ever driven while under the influence?

8. Have you ever tried to sneak alcohol, either when alone or at a party?

9. Do you ever drink alone?

10. Have you ever felt anxious or guilty about your drinking?

11. Have you ever made excuses or lied to hide your drinking?

12. Do you have a lot of friends who are heavy drinkers?

13. Do you feel uncomfortable or get angry when someone tries to discuss your drinking?

14. Do you have problems that are a direct or indirect result of your drinking?

15. Have you ever wondered if you are an alcoholic?

Although one "yes" response does not mean that you are an alcoholic, it is still a warning to think about the role that alcohol is playing in your life. If you answer "yes" to several questions, it is time to do more than think. It is time to talk to someone about your drinking. Do it today!

Someone I Know Drinks Too Much What Should I Do?

DON'T

1. Don't allow yourself to be lied to and to accept it as the truth. This only encourages the process of denial.

2. Don't accept promises. However, do expect any agreements that are made to be kept.

3. Don't lose your temper, thereby losing your effectiveness.

4. Don't do for problem drinkers what they need to do for themselves.

5. Don't allow yourself to be outsmarted or exploited.

6. Don't lecture, scold, praise, blame, threaten, argue, or use the "if you loved me" approach.

7. Don't pour out alcohol, hide bottles, mark bottles, or try to drink along with the problem drinker.

8. Don't regard this as a family disgrace.

DO

1. Do openly and honestly face facts.

2. Do accept alcoholism as a treatable disease.

3. Do discover the different sources of treatment in your area.

4. Do become knowledgeable about the disease of alcoholism and the disease of codependency

5. Do encourage the problem drinker to seek treatment.

6. Do seek treatment for yourself if you are a family member.

7. Do remember that recovery is often a long process requiring a great deal of patience.

8. Do offer understanding, support, and love in sobriety.

Adolescent Alcoholism

It is estimated that there are over *3 million* teenage alcoholics in this country today. Listed below are the four fairly predictable stages which the adolescent will go through in developing a dependency on alcohol, or some other substance:

Experimental Use:
Typically, adolescents begin their use out of curiosity, sometimes out of a desire to rebel against parents and society, and almost always in the company of friends. The use is often unplanned and is dependent upon one of the group being able to "get something." The thrill of doing something "sophisticated" and illegal is often part of the high. Because there is still very low tolerance to the substance, the high is easy to achieve.

Regular Use:
With regular use comes higher tolerance. More money will be involved, and false IDs may answer the problem of a steady supply. The adolescent may progress to hard liquor, but beer remains the most common teenage drink. Hangovers are accepted as a part of the scene, but as alcohol consumption increases, there is increased pride in being able to "handle it." "Blackouts" may begin to occur. One of the funniest jokes among a group is when one of them says, "Hey, did I do anything weird last night? I can't remember!" Trouble with parents increases as they begin to suspect what is happening. Preoccupation with use begins, and the next "party" is carefully planned and anticipated. Lying to parents and concerned friends about the extent of the drinking occurs frequently, and a lot of energy goes into fooling parents in particular. Non-drinking friends may be dropped with new drinking friends taking their place. The new drinking friends are frequently never introduced to parents.

Daily Preoccupation:

Drinking occurs several times a week now, with solitary and daytime drinking increasing. All school activities have been dropped, grades have dropped dramatically, and by now probably all non-drinking friends have been dropped. A steady supply of alcohol is kept hidden where no one else knows. Trouble with authority figures and parents increases due to truancies and legal problems, such as being picked up for minor consumption or driving under the influence. Adolescents may find themselves on probation about this time.

Dependency:

The adolescent is drinking daily now, often in the morning to get going and frequently at lunchtime. There is great confusion about what is normal behavior since being high has become normal. Feelings of guilt and self-hate increase, with thoughts of suicide increasing along with them. School has been dropped, jobs have been lost, but the problem continues to be denied. There is now loss of control over use.

The Excuses and the Realities
of Adolescent Alcoholism

But I'm a teenager.
So are at least 3 million teenage alcoholics and problem drinkers

But I drink only beer.
You get the same amount of alcohol in a 12 ounce can of beer, a 4 ounce glass of wine, or a 1 ounce shot of whiskey. The only difference is in how much you go to the bathroom.

But I never get really drunk.
High tolerance is a symptom of chemical dependency.

But I drink only on weekends.
You don't have to drink constantly to drink as an alcoholic.

But I never have blackouts.
Blackouts are only one of the symptoms of developing dependency, and they are not experienced by every alcoholic.

But I could quit anytime.
You could quit a hundred times and still start again. The only time that counts is the last time you quit.

But everyone else does it.
Do they?

Chapter 10

Children of Alcoholics

According to the National Association for Children of Alcoholics, there are an estimated 28 million children of alcoholics in this country today, with 7 million children aged 18 and younger. Over a third of all children of alcoholics end up marrying someone who is, or will become, an alcoholic. More than half of all alcoholics have at least one alcoholic parent.

Children of alcoholics are likely to suffer from learning disabilities, anxiety, eating disorders, stress related medical problems, compulsive achieving, chemical dependency, and suicidal tendencies. Children of alcoholics are also frequently victims of incest, neglect, and other forms of abuse. In most child abuse cases, alcohol is a factor. A disproportionate number of children of alcoholics become involved with the juvenile court system and later with adult court.

Children of alcoholics experience overwhelming feelings of shame, insecurity, and loneliness. They grow up feeling that something is wrong in their family, but since no one talks about it, they assume they are to blame. They think that if only they were better children, this wouldn't be happening. Children of alcoholics also grow up with the fear that something bad can happen at any time. They learn to expect erratic behavior and frequent crises because their environment is always potentially out of control. Later in life, many of them will have a strong need to completely control every situation because of their continuing fear that something terrible might happen at any time. Since they never know when the crying and shouting will erupt, they quickly learn not to invite friends to their house. It doesn't take long before they are isolated from other children their age.

Since the family denies that a problem exists, children of alcoholics also experience great confusion. Their senses say that something is wrong, but no one else seems to think so. Soon, children of alcoholics begin to question their own instincts. This often is carried into their adult life where they show a painful lack of confidence in their interpretation of situations and people. The adult child of an alcoholic often looks to others to determine what is and what isn't real, even though trust remains a very deep issue.

Children of alcoholics never know which side of the alcoholic they will see at the end of the day. Will it be the parent who smiles, laughs, hugs, and plays, or the yelling and screaming parent who drags them into the bathroom because socks were left on the floor? After years of having the trust that develops during the good times violated when the drinking begins, children of alcoholics soon decide that the only people they can depend upon are themselves.

Children of alcoholics often hear their nonalcoholic parent "cover" for the alcoholic by lying to others. The children's lies start as lies of protection also. Soon, children of alcoholics are lying much of the time. The lying behavior becomes so compulsive that children of alcoholics will often lie when it would be just as easy to tell the truth.

A reversal of the traditional roles for parent and child often takes place in the alcoholic home, with the parent becoming the child and the child becoming the parent. Children of alcoholics often find themselves in the difficult role of trying to take care of the drinking parent and younger brothers or sisters, while trying to meet their own needs as well. It is said that alcoholics don't have relationships. They take hostages. This is the experience of many children of alcoholics who come to feel that they are there only to take care of the alcoholic parent's needs. They become children without a childhood.

The emotional and the physical scars of children of alcoholics are many and deep. Cases of young children being traumatized by being left alone all night, or by having to hide food so they will have something to eat, or by being physically ill and not having anyone sober enough to notice are heartbreakingly common. Many children of alcoholics also suffer sexual molestation and other forms of physical violence by their alcoholic parent. It is estimated that half of all family violence occurs in alcoholic homes.

Because of the intolerable nature of their situation, children of alcoholics tend to experience what is called "psychic numbing." In order to survive their pain, they create a distance between what happens to them and how they feel. This distance is a buffer between themselves and their emotions, and it becomes an habitual response to painful situations.

Getting children of alcoholics to talk about what is happening to them is extremely difficult. Besides having learned early never to trust anyone, they have also probably been warned never to give away the secret of the family's alcoholism. Add to this their own personal sense of shame and guilt together with the emotional blocks they have built, and it is easy to understand their fear of confiding in others and their difficulty in expressing feelings.

The first and most difficult step toward recovery comes in breaking through the denial. Support groups for children of alcoholics are extremely helpful in encouraging them to lower the wall of resistance and denial that is so strongly in place. In a group of young people their own age who have also lived through very similar experiences, they will hear others talking about similar feelings. Suddenly it becomes clear they are not alone and their experiences did not happen to them because there was something wrong with them.

Children of alcoholics need to learn about the disease of alcoholism so they can understand the alcoholic parent's behavior and realize it was not their fault. They need to understand that the roles they adopted and the responses they made were normal ones for an abnormal situation. They need to express the long suppressed feelings of shame, guilt, confusion, anger, and terror. They need to begin reconstructing the past by reviewing it from their new perspective and knowledge of the disease of alcoholism. They need to develop a sense of themselves as individuals, rather than only seeing themselves as an extension of an alcoholic. They need to have some fun and to develop positive, nurturing relationships. They need to understand that eventually what they make of their lives is their own choice, and they no longer need to feel controlled by something they didn't understand.

In their developing awareness, children of alcoholics need to hear these messages:

> You did not cause it.
> You cannot control it.
> You cannot cure it.
> But you can learn to cope with it. Because you are
> not alone.

Indications That a Child May Be Living With Family Alcoholism

1. Frequent tardiness, especially on Monday mornings
2. Anxiety over getting home promptly at the end of the day
3. Being dressed improperly for the weather
4. Poor physical hygiene
5. Extreme maturity or immaturity
6. Avoidance of any conflict, or extreme argumentativeness
7. Isolation
8. Poor attendance
9. Frequent illness, especially stomach complaints
10. Fatigue and listlessness
11. Hyperactivity and difficulty concentrating
12. Emotional outbursts
13. Exaggerated concern with achievement
14. Extreme fear about situations involving contact with parents
15. Extreme negativism about alcohol
16. Unusual attention to alcohol in situations in which it is not the focus, such as in a movie which is not about drinking
17. Lingering by the teacher
18. Mention of a parent's drinking to excess on occasion
19. Mention of a friend who has a parent with a drinking problem
20. Strong concern about whether alcoholism can be inherited

Chapter 11
Grief

In all of our lives, there are many losses. Our losses range from those which we can accept in a relatively short period of time to those which may take years to assimilate. However, whether the loss is a "little death" or a deep and devastating one, it is important to recognize we are grieving.

Some of the "little deaths" we all experience are events such as trying out for a team and being turned down, having a relationship with a boyfriend or girlfriend end, or losing a best friend in a move to another city. In order to actually heal from *any* loss, we must move through the grieving process in order to come to terms with our new realities. The length of time that we grieve will be determined by how important the event is in our lives and also by how actively we enter the grieving process.

None of us probably ever experience greater pain than that of the loss of a loved one through death or in other ways. Grief becomes the price of loving. However, having the courage to be open to the pain of life is what allows us to be open to the joys of life as well.

Grief is the process we must all go through if we are ever to truly cope with our losses. If we have the courage to fully experience our pain, we will find it is the pain which heals itself. It is not possible to avoid the grieving process, only to delay it. When we try to deny feelings rather than to fully experience them, we only manage to lengthen our grief process and delay our healing. Then our feelings of grief simply surface at some later time, but in more complex and confusing ways.

We all work through our grief in our own individual ways and at our own pace. Some people cry continuously for days, while others may not cry for months or years. Some people make drastic changes in their lives, while others keep everything exactly the same. Whatever our personal style, the important thing is that we be allowed to grieve in our own way, fully experiencing the feelings of loss.

Probably the hardest part of being close to people who are grieving is that we tend to want to take away their pain *now*. This, of course, is neither possible nor even truly helpful. Probably the only thing that actually heals the pain of grief is time. Young people in particular often need help in understanding this. Though the intensity of grief lessens as time goes by, grief over major losses often lasts for several years. Young people who are still experiencing depression after a few months will sometimes wonder what is wrong with them. They feel they "should to be over it by now." Working to deal with feelings is what will speed the process, not working to deny them.

This means there actually is a great deal that others can do to help people who are grieving. By listening, we give the greatest gift we can offer. This is especially true when we listen in such a way that we give people permission to have the feelings they are experiencing. When we show that we accept and understand what people feel, we make no further demands on them. People who are grieving also frequently need to tell the same stories over and over again. It helps when there is a friend who understands that they are going to need to process these stories until they don't need to process them anymore.

Words will often fail us when we try to express what we feel for someone who is grieving. Then just being able to hold each other and cry together often helps more than anything else to take away the terrible feelings of pain and loneliness for awhile.

People will sometimes actually avoid someone who is grieving out of fear that they will say or do the wrong thing. Yet there is no such thing as the right thing to do! We need only to speak from the heart in order to send a healing touch into someone else's heart. If a person cries as a result of what we have said, no harm is done. Those are just a few more tears that are no longer locked inside the person.

People in grief need for those around them to accept where they are in the grieving process without pushing them to move faster than they can go. They will often work their way through the various stages only to go back time and again to previous stages. Part of the reason for this is that the full sense of loss is never felt all at one time. The pain is usually most intense for the six to eight weeks following the death. However, special days such as birthdays, Christmas, or the anniversary of the death, or things such as hearing an old special song can cause new waves of grief to wash over a person.

Often the worst time for people in grief occurs long after any support is thought to be necessary. By the time the protection of shock has worn off, they often find that no one is willing to talk about it any more, saying they need to quit dwelling on it. Without realizing it, other people actually do this to protect their own emotions, and they end up withdrawing support when it is still desperately needed. They do this because they can no longer bear to see their friend in pain and to feel there is nothing they can do. However, we must remember people are strong, and they will heal. As a friend, what we offer is not *doing* for them but *being there* as they search out their new paths.

Elisabeth Kübler-Ross has identified five stages that people in grief go through. While most people go through each of these stages, the length of time a person is in any stage varies for each individual. Also, people do not necessarily go through the stages in order.

The first stage is *denial*. The immediate reaction is, "No! There must be some mistake." The person thinks the accident report or the lab report must be wrong. This initial reaction of shock is the body's way of providing a cushion from the truth for a short while.

The second stage is *anger*. When denial is no longer possible, anger is expressed in questions of "Why them?" or "Why me?" People will sometimes lash out or blame others at this stage. Anger is a natural part of grief, and it helps when the people around the grieving person can accept and understand this.

The third stage is *bargaining*. Bargaining often takes the form of "if only" thoughts. "If only I had kept him here five more minutes, the accident would never have happened." Or, "If only you'll let me live, I'll donate the rest of my life to helping people."

The fourth stage is *depression*. As the reality sets in, the sense of loss deepens. The process of learning to say good-bye to someone, or to life, begins here. The depression often involves feelings of guilt, which need to be expressed.

The fifth stage is *acceptance*. This is best described as a re-conciliation or assimilation, rather than a recovery. We never totally get over a deep loss. Instead, we become re-conciled to it, and we learn finally to assimilate it into the new realities of our life. The day comes when we awaken feeling alive and happy, ready to get on with our lives even though we know we will never forget. For the person who is dying, this is a time of peaceful, quiet acceptance.

Grief is frequently made even more complicated by feelings of guilt. It is not unusual for both adults and children to blame themselves after a death or to feel guilty for things said or unsaid. Young children are particularly vulnerable because they do what is called "magical thinking." They believe that by thinking about something, they make it happen. At some time, most children have wished their parents would go away and leave them alone. When a parent dies, a child may feel responsible for the death and suffer in silence for years.

Also, our memories are especially difficult at first, causing some of our most vivid and painful feelings. Later these same memories become an important part of our healing because our memories keep a person alive inside us.

Life is for the living, and it sometimes helps to gently re-mind people that their loved one would not want them making it any more difficult on themselves than it has to be. Rather, they would want them to go on with the lessons of life—living, loving, learning, and growing.

Chapter 12

Rape

When most people hear the word "rape," they see images of a masked stranger lurking in a dimly lit parking lot or hallway waiting for a victim to appear. Although it is true that rape occurs in such situations, the chilling fact is that rape is also committed in well-lit homes and apartments, on weekend outings, and by people who are the victim's friends, neighbors, or dates.

It is estimated that:

Half of all rapes are committed by someone the victim knows

Half of all rapes occur in the daytime

Half of all rapes occur in the victim's home

The grim reality is over half of all rapes take place at times, with people, and in situations where the victim does not expect to be in danger. It is estimated one in four girls and one in six boys have been sexually molested by the age of 18. Although the rape victim will be referred to as a female here, it is important to recognize boys and men also are raped and the needs of anyone who has been raped are much the same.

Rape is not a crime of passion. Most rapists are married and have active sexual relationships, and almost all rapes are premeditated. Rape is a crime of power and violence in which the weapon is sex and the desire is to degrade and humiliate another human being.

Most women react first to the terror of being raped and later to the sexual aspects of the crime. If the important people around her, particularly her male friends and family members, become obsessed by the sexual nature of the crime, it only increases and complicates the guilt, confusion, and devastation she is experiencing. Because she is already overwhelmed, she is particularly vulnerable to the reactions of those around her.

Deep feelings of guilt are the strongest and most common reaction of a woman who has been raped. She keeps asking herself what it is about her that caused *her* to be the one raped. These feelings explain a great deal about why a very small percentage of all rapes are actually reported. While the embarrassment and humiliation are also reasons for not reporting, the sense of responsibility that many women experience works more than anything else to hold them back. Women need to understand that a man intent on raping chooses a victim because she is available, rather than for anything particular about her.

The physical needs of a woman who has been raped need to be dealt with as soon as possible. She needs to be checked for internal and external injuries, sexually transmitted diseases, and pregnancy. Hospital emergency rooms are usually best equipped to do the necessary tests. The woman should not shower, take a bath, or change clothes before receiving medical attention in order not to destroy important evidence.

A woman who has been raped is encouraged to report the incident since reporting does not commit her to taking further legal action. Because most rapists are repeat offenders, a report often serves to put a stop to the crimes. If a woman has filed a report, she then has the option later to decide whether or not she wants to prosecute.

Obviously a woman who has been raped has extremely strong emotional needs which also need to be met as soon as possible. A warm, concerned, and loving response from her family probably does more to help her than anything else.

She needs to feel believed, accepted, and loved. It will be important for her to talk about the assault, but this needs to happen only when she is ready. She also needs to be allowed to be as specific or as general as she chooses.

The victim of rape will go through all the stages of grief: denial, anger, bargaining, depression, and assimilation. The stage of depression is the time when a person actually begins to face the reality of the rape, and it can be the hardest stage to get through. Professional help at any time during the healing process can be extremely beneficial.

A rape victim will have many issues which will need to be addressed. The greatest of these will be that of guilt. A woman frequently needs to be reminded that she was not responsible for the rape. She needs to understand that _feeling_ guilty is not the same as _being_ guilty. Her guilty statements need to be challenged with questions such as: "If you blame yourself, then do you also blame other rape victims?" and "Would you blame yourself if you had been cheated or robbed?"

Trust becomes a major issue for most rape victims. They often move from one extreme to the other, going from trusting everyone to trusting no one. Although being more cautious is a positive development, a woman will often need to be encouraged to recognize the people whom she can trust. She needs to be assured that as her confidence in herself and her judgment returns, she will have a growing sense of her ability to decide whom she will trust.

Feelings of fear and vulnerability can seem overwhelming at times, and many rape victims experience flashbacks and nightmares. What she does _not_ need is to be made to feel helpless, however. Many times, fathers, husbands, or boyfriends respond by never letting the rape victim go anywhere alone after the rape. This only increases the woman's feelings of weakness, and it often increases her feelings of guilt as well. Instead of this over-reaction, it often helps the woman to take a course in self-defense or assertiveness training as a way to feel more empowered. If recurring dreams or nightmares continue, the rape victim can be helped to decide that she either will not have the dream anymore, or she will be the winner in the dream the next time. Helping her set aside a time each day to deal with her feelings often makes more than the nightmares go away.

Problems with self-esteem and with relationships are to be expected at first. A woman often feels sordid, dirty, or ruined. She needs to hear that rape is *not* a "fate worse than death." She needs to believe that her life is more important than her sexuality. She needs to recognize her strengths and positive qualities as a human being, rather than to define herself in a sexual way. However, it does need to be understood that she will have some problems with intimacy for awhile. These feelings usually pass with time if she has an understanding partner.

When feelings of anger begin to surface, it is a good sign of beginning recovery. If a rape victim is still not expressing anger, it is usually a sign of depression, with the anger turned inward and directed at herself. A rape victim needs to be encouraged and supported in her expressions of anger. She needs to write down her feelings, to talk about them, to increase her physical activity, or to do whatever gives release to her angry feelings. For some women, prosecuting the rapist is what allows them to finally let go of their anger.

As devastating as sexual assault is, it is not so devastating that a person cannot work through it. As with all traumatic experiences, when people have the loving support of family and friends and are able to talk about their feelings, a stronger person often emerges in the process. Many people have found that by helping others deal with similar situations, they are finally able to assimilate the experience and to regain a sense of control in their lives.

Chapter 13

Our Families, Our Selves

Our family experience is probably the single most significant influence in our lives, determining much of who we
are, who we become, what we value, and what we believe.
From our families, we either learn or don't learn how to
love, laugh, cry, play, work, share, earn, communicate, and
appreciate. Our family is our first group, and we carry what
we learn from this group out into all our other groups in
life. Because we are a part of many different types of
groups, at school, at work, with friends, and later with our
own families, we will continually use and test the lessons we
first learned with our families.

Many people find that the lessons they learned serve them
well in the world, and they work to continue those lessons.
Others find that the lessons they were taught do not serve
them well at all. These people will begin to unlearn old
lessons and to learn new ones in their continuing development. However, no matter what our experience, we all learn
from our families. We either learn how we want to be or
how we don't want to be. Either way, our families are there
to get us started. Where we go from there is up to us.

Few other groups ever test who we are like our families do.
It is one thing to get along with our friends, our teachers, or
our boss. It is an entirely different matter to learn to get
along with our family, sharing chores, bedrooms,
bathrooms, and growing room. In this setting, it is inevita-
ble that tensions and conflicts will arise. How we choose to
respond defines much about ourselves as individuals.

There will also never be another group that we are as likely to "should" on as our family. We tend to think that our family "should" do, and say, and be what will make us happiest. Rather than taking charge of changing ourselves when we want to be happier in our families, we tend to think that it is our family's job to change in order to make us happy.

As children, this attitude ignores a significant fact about our families. In most cases, *our* parents learned to be parents from *their* parents, and they often do not know another way to be parents. Strangely enough, this tends to be the case whether our parents were happy or unhappy with their parents. We can all learn important information about our parents by looking closely at their relationship with their own parents.

As parents, it helps to remember that children *will* make mistakes and that making mistakes and experiencing their consequences is an important part of each person's development. Although it is hard for parents to see their children make mistakes, what is important is that it is clear that people's worth in the family is not tied to their "success." Then, our families become an important support system in helping us to pick ourselves up, dust off the feelings of failure, and get on with it.

There actually *is* a secret to creating a happy family. The secret is for parents and children alike to treat each other the way they treat their friends and other people whose respect they value. For some families, the first step might actually be to treat each other with the courtesy they give to perfect strangers! Although this is not going to solve every problem in a family, it will prevent many new ones from starting. It will also create an environment in which problem-solving is much more likely to succeed. It is heartbreaking that this remains a secret in many families.

When we disagree with our friends, we usually do so clearly but with respect for their feelings and self-esteem. With our friends, we work to trust and to be trustworthy. With our friends, we learn to forgive and to be forgiven. With our friends, we show that we believe in them. With our friends, we give patience, affection, and love. With our friends, we enjoy openness, caring, support, and communication. When we learn to treat *our family* as we do our friends, in most cases our families become our friends—often our best friends.

Probably the single greatest issue in families is that of compromise. Of course, in most families there are some "non-negotiables," such as not staying out all night, not using alcohol or other drugs, not driving recklessly, and so on. With the exception of the "non-negotiables," though, one of the most powerful ways to acknowledge other human beings is to be willing to compromise with them. To compromise with other people demonstrates respect for their needs, recognition of the validity of their feelings, and a desire for both people to feel important. Since compromise means the settlement of differences by *mutual* concession, it is not a compromise when one person gives and the other one takes, only when both give.

No family can become stronger, happier, or healthier by focusing only on its problems and negative traits. Too often in our families we are aware only of what we don't like. We forget to acknowledge, or even notice, what we like and appreciate. It is important to be able to tell others what we want them to *keep* doing or *begin* doing, rather than only what we want them to *stop* doing.

Focusing on the positive in a person and in a family leads to the development of more that is positive. Positive qualities and mutual goals become something to strive for and upon which to build. A family that laughs together and has some fun each day, creates a balance for the stresses that *will* occur. A family that shares feelings and needs regularly learns to express appreciation as well as desired changes. A family that accepts and loves each other as they are finds people growing into what they can become.

Although it is true that some families are deeply troubled, most families that do not function well do so from a lack of awareness and commitment, rather than from a desire to cause pain. Because a chain is only as strong as its weakest link, most of us can help our families by becoming better family members ourselves. We can start by asking ourselves: What can I do to make this family something we will always treasure?

Chapter 14

Divorce:
The Disintegration of a Family

In the last 40 to 50 years, the American family has undergone vast changes:

Then:
Most families were part of a rural, farming community. Many people lived in the same community and the same house all their lives. People built their own houses and grew their own food on their own land. Work was something that was done at home.

Now:
Most families are part of an urban community. Most people leave home to go to work, trading services for money to purchase food and shelter.

Then:
Marriage was an economic necessity for both men and women. A man needed a wife to prepare and preserve food while he was in the fields every day. He needed a woman to bear and raise the children who would someday help him. A woman needed a husband to support and protect her.

Now:
Marriage is more often an emotional rather than an economic decision. It is a decision made out of a desire for happiness rather than one made out of necessity. Because of this, people now wait longer to marry and are more likely to end a marriage if it does not bring them happiness.

Then:
Divorce was highly unusual. Marriage was a sacred contract, and partners stayed together even when there was
unhappiness. Divorce was not economically possible for
most women because they could not support themselves or
their children. Society strongly disapproved of divorce, and
the stigma attached to divorced men and women made it
difficult for them to be accepted in society.

Now:
Divorce is commonplace and readily accepted by society. It
is predicted that close to half of all recent marriages will
end in divorce.

Then:
The only single parents were widows or widowers. Death
was the only thing that broke up families, and the widow or
widower usually quickly remarried.

Now:
Single parent families are rapidly becoming a normal childhood experience. Because of the high divorce rate and increasing numbers of children born to single women, it has
been predicted that by the year 2000, over half of all
children will live in a single parent household before they
reach the age of 18.

According to the U.S. Bureau of the Census, the rate of
divorce has increased in this country from less than one
divorce per 1,000 people in 1910 to five divorces per 1,000
people in 1985. However, the fact that divorce is one of our
common realities today does not prevent or minimize the
pain for those involved, especially for the children.

The environment in which the children lived before a
divorce will have a profound affect on them, whether it was
positive or negative. If the environment was filled with
open conflict long before the announcement of the divorce,
the children probably will already have developed some
coping problems. On the other hand, if the marriage
partners had long since given up on the relationship, there

may have been the illusion of peace within the family. In this case, both parents may have been quietly pursuing their own lives, rarely come together to fight or share in any way. However, this situation is also a very difficult one for the children. Because they do not recognize the apparent peace for what it really is, they often have more difficulty in accepting the idea of divorce.

Another factor that determines how well children cope with divorce comes in how the announcement is made. If the announcement of the divorce is made spontaneously and with no preparation, the children often experience increased fear and confusion because of the way in which they are told. Ideally, a decision to divorce needs to be communicated by both parents with the entire family together. However, it is important that this occurs only after the parents have anticipated the needs and can answer the likely questions of the children. It is much easier for children to deal with information than with what they will imagine.

Although children of divorced parents will experience different needs at different ages, there are some needs which are constant with all age groups. Children need to understand that no one parent is solely responsible for the divorce. They need to be allowed to believe in the worth of both parents and to maintain a consistent, loving relationship with each. They need to know that even though their parents have decided to divorce each other, their love for the children will last forever. They need to never be used as a pawn in any continuing battle between their parents. They need to be allowed to stay in familiar surroundings, attending the same school with the same friends. They need to be told clearly that in no way are they responsible for the divorce. They need to be allowed to mourn the loss of their parents as a couple, and they need to be allowed to express their grief and to deal with it at their own pace.

The age and developmental stages of children seem to be the most important factors in determining how they will respond initially to a divorce. How well they understand what is happening has a great deal to do with how they assimilate the experience in their lives. In general, younger children seem to have a more difficult time than the older ones, with the research seeming to indicate the younger the child the more severe the impact. Following are some of the responses and corresponding needs of children based on their developmental levels.

Preschool (3-5):
These children are frightened and confused, experiencing great anxiety. They often deny the reality of the divorce as a way of dealing with it. They will frequently develop eating and sleeping disturbances. Often they will regress to earlier, more immature behaviors such as thumb sucking or clinging. They show a general fearfulness but have particularly strong fears of punishment and rejection. They often imagine they will be sent away or replaced. They tend to feel guilty and to blame themselves for the divorce. This will sometimes manifest itself in the "too good child."

This age group needs strong reassurances they will be cared for and are loved. They need increased physical contact and comfort, and they need consistency in day to day routines and in discipline. They may need to hear repeated explanations of what the divorce will mean and what the arrangements will be. They will need help in understanding the connection between the divorce and all that is happening to them, such as feelings of sadness, nightmares, and so on.

Early School Age (6-8):
These children experience deep feelings of sadness and grief although they are less likely to feel guilty for the divorce. They feel confused, helpless, betrayed, deprived, and rejected. They experience strong feelings of anger but usually have difficulty expressing it. These children are torn by strong loyalty conflicts. They experience a deep insecurity, fearing the loss of the custodial parent as well as the absent parent. They have an intense desire for reconciliation, often having fantasies one day the absent parent will walk in and the family will be together again. They are old enough to understand what is happening without being old enough to have the skills to deal with it effectively.

This age group needs to be assisted in expressing their feelings directly and openly. They will need help in putting their feelings in perspective and in dealing with them. They need structure and consistency. Their reconciliation fantasies need to be recognized, and they need gentle assistance in accepting the finality of the divorce. They need to feel that they can love and enjoy both parents without feeling they will hurt the other parent. They need free and easy access to both parents, with regular visitations by the non-custodial parent.

Older School Age (9-12):
These children experience intense anger, feeling outraged at having to "lose" one of their parents. Because they tend to look at things rigidly, thinking in black and white terms, they will often blame and reject one parent. They may become very demanding, using temper tantrums and guilt to get what they want. They frequently choose tough or indifferent exteriors to cover their feelings of insecurity and vulnerability. They experience deep feelings of loneliness and rejection, as well as shame and resentment. They are sensitive to the feelings of others and become prone to worry, often becoming over-involved with the custodial parent.

This age group needs to have their anger acknowledged and to have their manipulation exposed openly but lovingly. They need to have a realistic appreciation of both their parents because this enhances their own feelings of self-esteem. They need to feel secure in day to day arrangements and to have continuity and consistency in their involvement with both parents. Because they often are afraid that in talking to one parent they will betray the other, they may need to talk to someone outside the family.

Adolescence (13-18):
These young people experience deep feelings of sadness, loss, and betrayal, and they often openly express their anger. They will sometimes act out their feelings through increased use of alcohol or other drugs, promiscuity, or delinquency. They frequently feel resentful at having to deal with yet another burden during a time when they already feel so burdened by life. They often feel shame and

embarrassment by what they see as their parents' failure, taking it as a personal failure. They also worry about the possible implications in their parents' divorce on their own future marriage. They feel concerned about money and the family's financial situation. They will often adopt a pseudomaturity, developing independence at a much earlier age. If their parents begin dating, they are also forced to recognize them as sexual beings.

This age group needs to be encouraged to fully express their feelings and fears, while being reminded that they are not extensions of their parents. They will frequently need to be urged to disengage from what is happening and to get on with their own lives. They need to be kept informed of all that is appropriate but never to be used as a confidant by one or both parents. Though they will undoubtedly be asked to take on more responsibility, they need not to be asked to become the absent adult or to feel responsible for one or both adults. They need limit setting and guidance in order to avoid over-reaction, and they need parents who continue to be parents, rather than becoming pals.

Divorce is a series of complex and on-going processes involving more factors than just the divorce itself in its affect on children. The degree of parental conflict has more affect on the children than whether the parents are married or divorced. Even after the divorce, how well the parents relate to each other determines the quality of the other family relationships. This is a critical factor because the best adjustment for children occurs in situations in which they have positive relationships with both parents. The new financial situation of the family is another critical factor for the children. A change in economics often means moving to a new location, and this is an additional factor that complicates the ability of children to adjust to a divorce.

While the difficulties for children in dealing with divorce cannot be minimized, children can deal successfully with divorce and can emerge as stronger people when their needs are met. If they are allowed to love and continue to be loved by every member of their family, their opportunities for growth can enrich their lives.

Chapter 15

Stepfamilies:
Families Learning to Walk in Step

The profile of the American family has changed dramatically in the last few decades. Although we still have the classic families which consist of a father, mother, and two children, those families are no longer the norm. We now have growing numbers of single parent families consisting of mother and children or father and children. Also in ever increasing numbers are our stepfamilies consisting of mother/stepmother, father/stepfather, and children/stepchildren.

Although some stepfamilies occur due to the death of one of the parents, most of our stepfamilies today are formed as a result of divorce. It is estimated close to 50 percent of marriages will now end in divorce. Most divorced people remarry and about half of these remarriages involve children. It is believed about one in every five children today has a stepparent.

Every family is different. It is important to understand the ways in which stepfamilies are different from biological families. The most significant difference is that the stepfamily is born from loss. It comes into existence due to a personal loss by every member of the stepfamily. The children will have "lost" one parent. At least one of the stepparents will have lost a partner. Even a previously unmarried stepparent will have lost any dream of having a traditional, biological family. *Every* person in the stepfamily may be grieving a personal loss.

Because people grieve at different rates, a remarriage will sometimes occur before children have resolved their grief and are ready to be a part of a new family. These children experience a double failure—failure to hold the first marriage together and failure to keep the second one apart.

While the parent and stepparent are also dealing with losses, they frequently grieve for a shorter period of time than children, especially when they wanted the end of the first marriage. Adults who are part of stepfamilies have chosen this way of life, and they will continue to choose it as long as it brings personal satisfaction. Children usually become a part of a stepfamily through no choice of their own, and they must cope with the situation whether it brings personal satisfaction or not. For the children, a remarriage can become yet another loss to be experienced.

Adding to the stress, many stepfamilies come together with the expectation that there will be "instant love" between the children, stepparents, and stepsiblings. Parents often will experience guilt, frustration, and feelings of rejection when instant love does not occur, never realizing that they are trying to achieve an impossible goal. Love takes time to develop, and it is enough at first if stepfamily members will work to enjoy and respect each other. The demand that the children call their new stepparent "Mom" or "Dad" comes from the desire for instant love and for the normalcy it represents. However, this kind of pressure is much more likely to develop resentment than love among stepfamily members.

Each person also brings different past histories, values, and traditions to the stepfamily. In order to blend two or more ways of doing things, the stepfamily must develop new approaches out of old memories, loyalties, and belief systems. This includes everything from how holidays are celebrated ("*We* open our presents on Christmas morning." "Well, *we* open ours on Christmas Eve.") to how family members work together and relate to each other. The new stepfamily will have to decide who does which chores and how the distribution of chores is arranged. They will have to decide how much freedom the children will be given and what they will be allowed to do. They will have to decide whether children earn their spending money or are given an allowance. They will have to decide whether people clean their plate or just eat what they want, whether they work first or play first, which television shows are watched on which nights, and so on. One of the most difficult new questions is who disciplines whom in the family, how, and for what.

Resolving these questions is made even more complicated by the fact the children are frequently members of more than one household. There is usually a biological parent living somewhere else who will have to be taken into consideration. Because of custody and visitation arrangements, the stepfamily members who are actually present at any given time changes frequently. The boundaries of the new family become blurred for everyone.

Stepfamilies also tend to experience more "triangles" than biological families. The children's relationship with their own parent will be of longer duration than the relationship of the parent and stepparent. While there is an emotional and legal bond between the children and the biological parent and between the parent and stepparent, there is no legal and often no emotional bond between the children, stepparent, and stepsiblings.

Children in stepfamilies often experience changes in their position in the family, such as going from being the oldest child to being the youngest. A child can also go from being the only girl or boy in the family to being one of several. Because there can be abrupt changes in family size, children often find themselves sharing space and possessions with new stepsiblings as well.

Probably the most accurate single word description of a stepfamily is "complex." Many stepfamilies do not realize the problems they encounter are due in large part to the complexities and uncertainties of their family system. Many stepparents feel that there must be something wrong with them if trouble develops in the stepfamily. This seems to be especially true for those who have already had a first marriage end in divorce. Because they cannot deal with the possibility of what they think of as another failure, they try to ignore the trouble, not realizing it may be due to unrealistic expectations and lack of awareness.

In order to develop identity as a stepfamily, there is much that needs to happen. The stepfamily members will each need to mourn their personal loss by being allowed to express their feelings, needs, and wishes. They will each need to participate in negotiating and establishing new traditions. Frequent family meetings can be extremely helpful in providing an effective way to find positive solutions for disagreements. These meetings can also be used to explain or discuss the complexities of stepfamily systems. While the old loyalties need to be maintained, new alliances and friendships within the stepfamily need to be formed. The new stepfamily needs to look toward its future together and to determine its mutual goals.

While stepfamilies tend to be more stressful than intact, biological families, many adults and children alike find a special satisfaction and sense of accomplishment in their stepfamilies. Often people in a stepfamily have become more aware of the precious and fragile nature of relationships, learning to work much harder to maintain them. There is a deep sense of growth and strength that comes from being a part of a family system that began with loss and moved toward personal gain for each of its members.

Chapter 16

Dreams:
The Mirror of Your Mind

Dreams are fascinating experiences. They can be humorous, beautiful, terrifying, weird, sad, or they can help us solve a problem. If you have ever had the experience of going to sleep trying to solve a problem and then dreaming the solution, you have probably long been convinced of the value of dreams. However, no matter what a person's experience with dreams has been, almost everyone is intrigued with dreams and with what they mean.

Interest in dreams has continued to increase in this country for several decades. However, some societies have studied and used dreams for centuries. One example of this is an isolated jungle tribe known as the Senoi, who live in the rain forests of the Malay Peninsula. The Senoi value their dreams as important sources of guidance and knowledge. Every morning on awakening, the family gathers to discuss their dreams of the previous night. They pay a great deal of attention to the messages in their dreams. For example, if the Senoi have a dream in which they are attacked by a fellow tribesman, they will go to the person that same day to discuss the dream, making sure there are no unresolved conflicts. Scientists who have studied the Senoi say they live in a culture with no war and little or no violence or mental illness.

You may respond to this by saying, "That sounds wonderful, but there's just one problem. I never dream!" Dream research has now clearly established that everyone dreams on the average of three to five times a night, or between one thousand and two thousand dreams in a year. The most significant factor in whether we remember our dreams seems to be *how much we want to remember our dreams!* Dream researchers also have found that "nonrecallers" tend to be highly rational, analytical thinkers while "recallers" tend to be more open, flexible, and "feeling" thinkers. For example, engineers tend to recall fewer dreams than artists. In our society, men tend to recall fewer dreams than women.

People sometimes wonder if it is worthwhile, or even dangerous, to delve into dreams. Our dreams are messages *from* us *to* us. They are messages that relate to how we are feeling and what we need to be doing. They often point out important information we have overlooked or ignored in our busy schedules. In a book by Harmon Bro titled, *Edgar Cayce On Dreams,* Edgar Cayce is quoted as saying, "The alternative to recalling and interpreting dreams is not always pleasant. Individuals cannot expect to drift forever. If they do not puzzle out their identity, and the direction of their lives by the aid of their dreams, then they may be brought, by the relentless action of their own pent-up souls, into some crisis which requires that they come to terms with themselves. It may be a medical crisis. It may be the end of a marriage or of a job. It may be depression...." Encouraging our dreams is not where the risk lies. The risk may lie in ignoring them.

Dream recall is a talent that some people seem to have naturally. For others, it is much more difficult. However, with desire and dedication, most people can vastly improve their dream recall by using techniques such as the following:

1. **Keep a dream diary.**
   Keep a notebook, pen, and flashlight, or a tape recorder, next to your bed. This signals your subconscious mind of the seriousness of your interest, and it also allows you to record your dreams without getting up. The more movement you make after recalling a dream, the more likely you are to lose the memory of the dream.

2. Date the entry each night.

Record the day's date and write "Dream 1" under it. This again signals your subconscious mind that not only do you expect to remember a dream, you expect to remember more than one! Also, having the date of each dream can be important later as you work to understand your dreams and their relationship to things that happened during the day.

3. Give yourself a pre-sleep suggestion.

Tell yourself that you are going to remember your dreams. Once you have relaxed in bed, say "I will recall my dreams when I wake up." Or, "I will wake up after each one of my dreams." Concentrate on what you are saying and repeat it several times before you fall asleep.

4. Record all dreams.

Record any dreams immediately upon awakening. It is important to do this the moment you awake since dreams have a tendency to fade away quickly. No matter how vivid a dream seems in the middle of the night, usually by morning most or all of it will have slipped away. Also, don't assume that a dream isn't important enough to record. What seems trivial in the middle of the night may take on new importance as you consider it in the morning. It also is important not to have any preconceived ideas about what a dream is. If you awaken with anything at all in mind, a thought, an impression, or a song, write it down.

5. Write a full description of your dream.

Record all the details of your dream, writing this description in the present tense. This will often help you to recapture the experience of the dream in the morning. Take special note of your mood upon awakening. This often helps in interpreting the message of a dream. Look for things such as: the setting of the dream, the people, the action, the dialogue, any unusually vivid color, and especially your feelings.

6. **Begin a new dream entry.**

   If you record a dream in the middle of the night, write "Dream 2" under your first dream, and then "Dream 3" under the second one, and so on. Often, dreams of the same night will relate to the same issue, but they will each approach it in a different way. One dream will often shed new light on another dream, and together they provide a great deal of information.

7. **Do an analysis of your dream.**

   Go back through the dream and identify all the symbols of the dream and their meaning to you. Consider the relationship between the dream and the events of the previous day. Even if you are unable to identify any relationship, record the highlights of the previous day for later use. If you dream about a television show you watched that night, do not assume that your dream was just a rehash of that show. This is usually just the symbolism that your dream used to bring you its message. Dreams do not come to tell you something you already know. They come to show you something you have not fully realized. Dreams are always triggered by something on our minds or in our hearts.

8. **Talk about your dreams.**

   Nothing makes such interesting breakfast conversation as a discussion of the previous night's dreams! Talk to your family or friends sometime during the day about your dreams. You will often discover a new understanding of a dream while trying to explain it to someone else. Also, this is another way of signaling your subconscious mind that you are taking this process seriously. Eventually you will begin to experience exciting new insights.

Learning to understand and interpret your dreams can be the most frustrating part of studying dreams at first. However, it usually doesn't help to rush out and buy a copy of something called *1,000,000 Dream Symbols Interpreted For You* by someone named I. Will Showyouhow. Although some understanding of dream symbolism helps in interpreting your own dreams, *you* are the person who is best qualified to interpret them. While it is often helpful to have people who know you well suggest a possible meaning in a dream, it is important to realize that most people will interpret *your* dream the way they would interpret it if it were *their* dream. The same symbol often does not mean the same thing to two different people, and it may not even mean the same thing every time with the same person. The thing to remember is this: if the explanation feels right, then it probably is. If it doesn't feel right, it's not. Since *you* are the one who produced your dream, on some level you already know what it means!

The reason we dream in symbols is because we think in symbols. If someone asks you, "Who is your English teacher?" you will picture your teacher in your mind before you ever respond. Some of the first types of communication came in the form of drawings on cave walls, and the symbols that were used often had a universal understanding or application. The saying, "A picture is worth a thousand words," certainly applies here. Symbols are a clear and concise way to communicate, once we learn to speak the language.

In most dreams, the dreamer actually plays most or all of the parts. The characteristics of the other players in the dream are often actually the characteristics of the dreamer. In dreams, we meet ourselves in a lot of different roles and disguises. For example, sometimes the "evil villain" in a dream will be played by a stranger. This can be a message that we are keeping ourselves unaware of some characteristic in ourselves. In addition to playing most parts in our dreams, we also dream primarily of ourselves. Although a few dreams may relate to loved ones or world events, most dreams are centered around ourselves. Dreams are our mind's way of processing what we are doing, who we are becoming, and where we are going.

Dreams can be interpreted both literally and symbolically. Always look for a literal meaning or warning in a dream as well as for the symbolic meaning. For example, if you have a dream in which your teeth fall out, it might be advisable to see a dentist if you haven't been in some time. Or, if you dream of eating lots of fruit and vegetables, perhaps you should take a closer look at your diet. Remember, though, that dreams will often carry a message on *both* a literal and a symbolic level.

In analyzing your dreams symbolically, you may find it helpful to make two columns on a piece of paper. Label the left column: Dream symbols. Label the right column: What I associate with this symbol. Then, go through your description of the dream and in the left column list all the symbols you recognize. In the right column, list all your associations with that symbol. The meaning of the dream often becomes apparent at this point.

Our dreams have an uncanny way of using puns, body language, slang, or our favorite expressions as a way of communicating with us. If you dream that you are wearing a pair of pants that keeps getting tighter and tighter, the message might be that "you are getting too big for your britches." Or, if you are running along a dock but your ship pulls away before you get there, the message might be that "you are missing the boat." However, if you dream that you have lost some money, look first to see if you have lost your wallet but *also* ask yourself if you have lost some of your values.

Following are some dream symbols and their *possible* meanings:

Car: physical body, way of getting around in the world
Falling: loss of status, fear of failure
Flying: rising above it all, being on top of the world
Nudity: feeling vulnerable or exposed
Nudity (but no one notices): some personal disclosure is really no big deal
Taking an exam: being put to the test
Key: solution, new approach
Living room: daily activities
Hallway: place of transition or change
Closed door: negative attitude
Alarm clock ringing: warning

False teeth: false or angry words
Having a large mouth: talking too much
Eye: "I" or insight
Right side: right way
Blindness: refusal to see
Going on a hike: life

As you progress in the art of working with your dreams, you may want to begin developing your own dream dictionary, containing your personal dream symbols. The language of your dreams has only one dictionary, and that is the one written by you. If your dreams sometimes seem illogical, this is usually because you remember only fragments of the dream or because the dream relates to something illogical about yourself. Or, it may be you have not yet learned to speak this language of the heart and mind.

People sometimes experience the same dream repeated several times over a period of months or years. These dreams will usually continue to repeat themselves until the dreamer understands the message and acts upon it. Nightmares are sometimes an example of our dreams having to take desperate measures to get our attention. There are exceptions to this, of course, such as nightmares we might have with a fever. Usually, though, if our dreams cannot get our attention in subtle ways, they will get our attention in ways we cannot ignore. However, when we show a desire to open ourselves to our minds and hearts, the doors are opened to a treasure house which will enrich our lives beyond description.

Peer Helping Post-Test

For each of the statements below, write what you feel would be a helpful response to a person who had made that statement to you:

1. "I really hate this school and this town! I didn't want to move—especially to this place. I can tell this is going to be a lousy year."

2. "I can't believe it! She did it to me again! I told my friend something I didn't want anyone else to know, and now it's all over the school. I'm going to find a way to get even with her."

3. "I just found out that my best friend was killed by a drunk driver last night. And to make things worse, the last time we talked, we had an argument. I was going to try to settle things this weekend."

4. "When my dad drinks, he and my mom start arguing. They have these terrible fights. What should I do?"

5. "I'm failing my English class, and if I don't pass it, I won't graduate. My parents are always on my back about getting good grades so I'll get a scholarship. I think I'm going to lose my job, and now I seem to be fighting with my friends all the time. Sometimes I'm really not sure life is worth it."

Unit IV
Support Group Program

Chapter 17
Group Leadership

As a group leader, you are initially the most influential part of the group, and your responses will do much to determine how productive the group becomes. At first, it is likely that both you and the group members will be nervous and uncertain as to what to expect from the group process. By openly acknowledging your feelings, you will make it easier for others to do the same. If you wish to see members of your group risk meaningful disclosure, then it must begin with you.

Any anxiety among group members that is due to the new-ness of the experience will pass relatively quickly. However, if anxiety is due to a fear of inadequacy or a fear of rejection, it will take increased patience and understand-ing by the group leader to get the group past this point. The group leader will need to remember that when people feel anxious, they tend to fall back on social behaviors that have worked for them in the past—being cool, being silly, being silent, being superior, or being confused. It is not until they learn they can trust the group that they will try being honest instead.

Because people need and want to be accepted for who they are, group members find themselves faced with the risk of sharing some part of themselves. For most group members, early self-disclosure will tend to be rather tentative. While there may be a lot of talking within the group, most people will not yet be saying anything significant about themselves. However, if this remains a characteristic well into the life of the group, the group leader needs to recognize that fear of rejection may *still* be interfering with the progress and development of the group.

One of the aspects of group work that is most difficult for many leaders is silence within the group. It helps to remem-ber silence is a natural and productive part of the interac-tion of individuals and groups. Usually only one person talks at any one time. Silence is just a time when one more person than usual is quiet. The focus needs to be on the meaning of the silence, rather than on the silence itself. Is it the silence that occurs while people are deciding how they want to respond? Is it the silence that comes when people don't understand what is expected of them? Is it the silence that follows a touching experience? Or, is it the silence that comes when people are experiencing emotions they are afraid to express?

Another important function of the group leader is to help the group members relate to each other. When people feel accepted by others who have had similar feelings and ex-periences, two very important things happen. One is people begin to realize they are not the only ones who have had those feelings and experiences. This awareness often allows them to let go of the secret fear there must be something wrong with them. The other is a special feeling of trust and understanding that begins to develop within the group. If this feeling is nurtured through interaction and comfortable disclosure, it often leads to a special feeling of closeness within a group. This is referred to as *group cohesion*. Although it does not have to be present for members to benefit from the group experience, it does usually accelerate and deepen the growth that occurs.

Groups are very powerful and carry great potential for change. In our society, people tend to be taught at an early age to withhold and deny their feelings. Messages such as, "Big boys don't cry," or "You're such a baby" come at an early age. At least for awhile, most people respond to these messages by pretending to be what is expected of them. This leaves people denying a large part of themselves. By being part of a group, people have the opportunity to interact with others in more honest ways. Group also provides an opportunity to observe different ways of behaving and of expressing feelings. In group, people can become clearer on how others perceive the things they do, and they can choose to develop more effective ways of being. Because we all behave in terms of the way we see ourselves, group offers an opportunity for people to see themselves in more accepting and positive ways.

In a group experience, people also have the opportunity for giving as well as receiving help. This becomes an important function of the group. People are frequently much more generous in their support of others than of themselves. Most people have had the experience of saying something to others that they really need to be saying to themselves. They may suddenly realize the connection for themselves in what they are saying, or a member of the group may bring it to their attention. In group, as in life, giving becomes receiving, and receiving becomes giving.

As members become more involved in the group process, they begin to place more value in working on their relationships outside of the group. Group members begin to take "out into the world" what they have experienced and learned within the group. Group becomes a place to practice more effective behaviors, with the ultimate goal being that its members will assimilate them into the framework of their lives.

As bonds form within the group, the members develop an increasing concern for each other. Individual differences are respected and appreciated for the opportunities they offer within the group. As group members become better able to understand each other, they also become more skilled at understanding themselves.

A higher degree of personal risk-taking and a greater depth of personal exploration and disclosure begins within the group. The atmosphere becomes noticeably warmer and more relaxed. Group members feel comfortable laughing or crying together, knowing they have the support and encouragement of the group. There is a growing commitment to growth among members. This leads the group to become more accepting and confrontive, thereby more productive.

Because groups offer huge potential for growth and change, they can be one of the most exciting ways to work with people. The most functional groups often develop to the point where roles within the group become fluid, with leaders becoming followers and followers becoming leaders. At its best, the group provides a place where its members learn more about who they are and who they want to become. They come to understand that different people will respond to them in different ways. In experiencing the acceptance of a group, members grow in their acceptance of themselves. This frees them to focus on learning to live more effectively and finding more satisfaction and joy in their relationships and lives.

Stages in the Life of a Group

Stage I: Checking it Out

Characteristics:

The group members simultaneously are drawn to the group and frightened by it. They tend to either "wait and see" or to test out the group. Although there is a desire for intimacy, there is also resistance to discussing anything personal. Most discussion is of the past or the future, and the "here and now" is avoided.

Group Leader Tasks:

Accept and welcome all group members. Invite trust and confidence by displaying openness and honesty. Answer all questions fully and demonstrate enthusiasm and positive expectations for the group process. Provide structured activities by which members can begin to know each other.

Stage II: Where Do I Fit?

Characteristics:

Some group members may attempt to define and establish a role for themselves within the group. This may lead to the establishment of a hierarchy. Scapegoating of some members may occur as other members work to feel more secure in their position.

Group Leader Tasks:

Establish the worth of all group members through your interaction with them. Provide a safe environment in which people are protected from attack, rejection, or unnecessary pain. Help group members focus on their commonalties rather than their differences. Provide opportunities for the group members to learn to appreciate and understand each other.

Stage III: Getting Involved

Characteristics:
As trust and acceptance are established, group members begin to reveal themselves and to explore their issues. Personal risk-taking is recognized and acknowledged by the group, and self-disclosure becomes more comfortable. Members often begin to identify as a "family," sometimes establishing their own traditions.

Group Leader Tasks:
Provide support and encouragement as members risk becoming known to the group. Help members understand and accept their feelings as they begin to assimilate their experiences. Allow the group to take more responsibility for its direction while providing leadership if the group gets sidetracked.

Stage IV: Building Bridges

Characteristics:
Communication within the group becomes deeper and more meaningful. Members recognize each other as unique individuals, and uniqueness is appreciated and accepted. Feelings of closeness are openly expressed even as feedback and confrontation are valued. The group may experience cohesion, with members actively providing support, acceptance, and affection for each other. The beginnings of change occur within the group members.

Group Leader Tasks:
Encourage and assist group members in transferring what has been learned during the group into their personal relationships, while providing a safety net of support as they risk new behaviors. Continue to develop and expand the emotional bridges between group members.

Stage V: Letting Go

Characteristics:

As a group experience comes to a close, group members react in many different ways. Although some group members are able to savor the experience right up to the end, others deal with the end of the group by denying that it was ever important in the first place. Some group members will not accept that the group is ending, insisting that the members will always be as close as they are now. Some groups regress to earlier stages, moving apart prematurely. Other groups help each other in preparing to move on.

Group Leader Tasks:

Help the group members identify ways they can extend this group experience. Provide support systems by sharing phone numbers or by identifying other possible group experiences or community resources. Plan a special last group session, perhaps with individual "awards" or some other type of celebration. Help the group to evaluate its experience and encourage individual group members to determine their goals and direction.

Tips for Group Leaders

1. **Model the behaviors you want to see in your group.** Set the tone and teach by example. Demonstrate warmth, acceptance, caring, and interest in each of your group members.

2. **Keep the group sitting close together and in a circle.** Ask the group members to sit in a circle as a way to increase their involvement with each other. Then each person is in the front row, so to speak, and in a position of equal importance and involvement.

3. **Give recognition.** Learn each person's name and use it. If you forget a name, ask. Continually watch to see that the members of the group know each other's names.

4. **Have a plan for the group session.** Always come to the group with an activity or a discussion topic for that session. However, don't become rigid in your plans. Be flexible in allowing a different direction to be set when

the needs of group members surface. The main value of group activities is that they provide a framework in which members can get to know each other and to become more comfortable in revealing themselves. However, the purpose of the group is to give its members a place where they can talk about their lives—how they feel, what they are experiencing, and what they need.

5. **Be patient.** Understand that the group process may be a new experience for your group members. Concentrate on developing trust and a high level of comfort among group members. Allow for silence within your group. Remember that group members will need a few moments to decide how they want to respond to questions or as they search for the words to express themselves.

6. **Encourage everyone to participate.** Even if group members continually "pass" during a group discussion, continue to invite them to share thoughts and experiences. Watch body language for clues to times when a normally quiet member is ready to participate. Avoid having one or two members dominate the group discussion by saying, "Thank you for sharing with us. Now let's hear what some of the other group members would like to add."

7. **Encourage group members to interact with each other.** Avoid being the answer source. Rather than responding to every statement or question, instead say, "What do the rest of you think?" Observe the process of communication within your group. Whom do people look at when they talk? Who talks, how often, and for how long? Who responds to, or interrupts, whom?

8. **Keep the focus on the person speaking until that person is finished.** Avoid letting other group members take the focus away from someone who is talking. After a group member makes a statement, other group members will often respond by saying, "I've had *exactly* the same thing happen to me, and I...." Teach

your group to focus on the person who is speaking until that person has completely expressed feelings, explored possibilities or connections, and perhaps identified a new direction. After adequate time has been given to the person speaking, it is *then* of great value for other group members to share similar experiences.

9. **Help group members see the similarities in their experiences and feelings.** Notice when someone seems to be identifying with feelings being expressed by another group member. Encourage that person to talk about it when the first person is finished.

10. **Avoid asking "why?"** Questions of "why" lead to analyzing behavior rather than to dealing with feelings. Instead, ask questions such as "What were you feeling when you did that?" or "What do you think you got out of doing that?"

11. **Focus on feelings.** Go from experience to feelings by asking questions such as, "When that happened, how did you feel?" Pay as much attention to tone of voice and body language as to the actual words used. Accept all feelings as valid without any labeling, such as good or bad.

12. **Understand the value and purpose of group work.** Although groups are frequently uplifting experiences, they can be sad and heart-rending as well. No real value comes from being in a group that will not deal with topics that are "too depressing." This attitude only forces group members to hold inside what they came into the group to express! Help your group understand truly uplifting experiences come as a result of releasing old, painful feelings or in being a part of helping others do so.

13. **"WRAP" during each group session.** Make sure each group session contains these elements:

    Warm-up or energizer
    Review of the last group session
    Activity or group discussion
    Process of the group session

Giving (and Receiving) Feedback

One of the most important functions of groups is to provide appropriate and helping feedback to its members. Some of the most important information people can receive from others, or give to others, consists of feedback about behavior. Receiving feedback is like having someone hold a mirror so that we can better observe the consequences of our actions. Feedback is a special kind of communication that helps people become more aware of what they do, how they do it, and how it affects others.

Here are some guidelines for giving effective feedback:

Focus feedback on the behavior rather than on the person.
Effective feedback refers to what people *do* rather than to what you think they *are*. It is more effective to say, "That is the third time you have interrupted me today," rather than, "You are a loudmouth and don't care about anyone else!"

Focus feedback on observation rather than on interpretation.
Observations refer to those things people see or hear while interpretations refer to their own conclusions. So, it is more helpful to say, "You are very quiet today," than to say, "You are very depressed today."

Focus feedback on behavior during a specific, recent situation.
Feedback is most meaningful when it is given in specific terms using examples. The value of feedback is also much greater when it comes as soon as possible, and appropriate, after the event. This keeps it free of the distortion of time, helping to avoid disagreements on what did or did not happen. Therefore, it is more effective to say, "Last week when we were discussing group guidelines, it seemed like you thought my ideas were stupid whenever I disagreed with you," rather than saying, "You are too bossy in group!"

Focus feedback on sharing ideas and information rather than on giving advice.

When ideas and information are shared, it is expected people will decide for themselves how, or if, the information can best be used. When advice is given, the implication is that this is what a person "should" do. So, it is more helpful to say, "At first, I didn't like to talk in the group because I wasn't sure how people would react. But after talking a couple of times, I have found the people in this group to be really understanding," rather than saying, "You should talk more during group."

Focus feedback on its value to the recipient.

The purpose of feedback is to provide information which may be helpful to people or may improve your relationship with them. Feedback is never an excuse to "dump" on someone. Also, it is often a good idea to verify your feedback was received the way it was intended. One way to do this is to have people rephrase what you said to see if "what they heard is what you meant." During group, it sometimes helps to check with others on the accuracy of the feedback. Is it one person's impression or an impression shared by others?

It is important to realize that feedback sometimes tells us as much about the person giving it as it tells us about ourselves. Just because a person says it does not make it so. The strength in receiving feedback is in being open to the truth of what is said, while disregarding that which feels inaccurate. It also is in being open to another person's perception even if it is not our own, as this can lead to greater self-awareness and understanding.

Giving (and receiving) feedback requires genuine concern, courage, and respect for ourselves and others. When we learn to give it and receive it effectively, it improves our relationships and how we feel about ourselves.

Ground Rules for Group Sessions

1. Everything that happens or is said in this group is confidential and is to "stay in the group." If people want others to know something about them, *they* will tell them!

2. Everyone has the right to "pass" on any question or activity. If you pass frequently, it will keep you from being an active part of the group. Your reason for passing needs to be clear to you. You may find communicating this reason helps to keep you feeling close and involved with the group. If you decide to pass, let the group know if you would like them to come back to you later.

3. It is your right to speak freely and openly. No one needs permission to speak in the group. At the same time, it is also important to respect each person's right to talk without interruption and to see each person has an equal share of the available time.

4. Use "I" statements to express yourself during the group sessions. When people are uneasy about expressing their feelings, they will often describe them as if they belong to someone else. This leads to a lack of ownership of feelings. Rather than saying, "People don't like to talk in front of a group," say, "I am uncomfortable when I talk in front of a group."

5. Concentrate on speaking directly to people when you talk. Instead of saying, "John never pays attention when anyone talks," look at John and say, "John, I don't think you show respect for other people when they talk."

6. Be aware of feelings in the group. Work to recognize your feelings and to help others do the same. Because we tend to "stuff" our feelings in so many other situations, we will give special attention to feelings in this group.

7. Avoid making judgments of other people. It is hard enough learning to be ourselves without having others put us down.

8. Learn to give effective feedback. Focus on a person's behavior and your response to it rather than on your interpretation or evaluation of the person.

9. Demonstrate that other group members are important by listening carefully when they talk and by working to understand what they say.

10. Decisions made by the group require group consensus, meaning that everyone in the group must find the decision acceptable and be willing to support it.

11. We are here to be supportive of each other. Killer statements or put-downs of any kind will not be tolerated, whether they are directed at others or at yourself.

12. Decide to be at group each time and on time. When you are not here, it leaves a gap that cannot be filled by anyone else. Also, being late interrupts the group process, and everyone is affected.

13. Everyone who is here belongs here and is welcome.

Support Group Confidentiality Contract

My signature on this contract is my word that I will maintain confidentiality in everything that is said by any member of this group or that happens with any member of this group.

If I break or am aware of a break in confidentiality, I agree to abide by the following rules and consequences which have been established by my group:

Rules and Consequences:

_____

Group Member Signature

_____

Date

Chapter 18

Group Activities

One of the most rewarding and exciting experiences a person can have is to be a part of a personal growth group. Groups are a very powerful part of our lives, teaching us that as we learn to function effectively in groups we also learn to function more effectively in our lives.

The activities in this chapter will help your group move from trust building through the stage of acceptance and understanding and into that of mutual support and personal growth.

Phase I:
Building a Foundation for Trust

Activity 1
Getting to Know Each Other
and
What is This Group All About Anyway?

Introductions:

Have group members introduce themselves by giving their name preceded by an adjective which starts with the same letter or sound, for example, "Christmas Carol." Ask the group members to choose an adjective that tells something important about who they are, what they do, or how they feel. For example, "I chose Christmas Carol because I believe that if we all would approach life with the generosity, concern for others, and joy in giving that we show at Christmas, this would be a much happier world." The next person gives an adjective/name and explanation, and then repeats in order all the adjective/names of the group members. This continues around the circle until the last person gives an adjective/name and then repeats the adjective/name of every member of the group.

Or, after introductions have been made, ask people to describe themselves with two truths and a lie. For example, "I like to snow ski, I like to play chess, and I like to cook." The group then has to guess which are the two truths and which is the lie.

Then ask group members to form pairs, getting with a person whom they know least. Instruct the members that they each will have three minutes to learn as much as possible about their partners. When time is called, they will introduce their partners to the group.

Schedule:

Make sure the group members are clear on where and when they will meet each time. Discuss details, such as taking roll. If group members will miss class time to be in group, suggest some positive strategies for handling this responsibility. Also, decide if you will send reminders.

Group Discussion:

Group members will want to know more about what they can expect from being in the group. Make a statement like the one that follows, phrasing it in your own words:

"This group is a place where we can get to know other people and ourselves better. Before any of us will feel comfortable in opening up to this group, we will have to believe we can trust each other. Our most important job at the beginning will be to show we can be trusted and to work at learning to trust the other members of the group."

"To make it easier to get to know each other, we will have activities planned at first. Activities are not really what this group is all about. They are just a way to get us started. What this group is really all about is having a place where we can talk about our lives—how we feel and what we need."

"It is so special when a group of people really care what happens to each other and are supportive of each other. In groups like this, people often find that there are others who have had similar problems or experiences and can understand how it feels."

Ask if there are any questions. Spend whatever time is necessary to answer them thoroughly.

Ground Rules for the Group:

Explain that because you want the group to be a good experience for everyone, you have some ground rules that everyone will be expected to follow.

Give a copy of the "Ground Rules For Group Sessions" to the group members. After they have had time to read them and ask questions, ask if there are any other guidelines they would like to have added to the list. If there is consensus on a suggested ground rule, add it to the list also.

Go around the circle and ask people to talk about:
(1) the rule that is most important to them, and
(2) the rule that they will have the most trouble following.
Ask if there is anything the group can do to help with this.

Confidentiality:

Talk about how important confidentiality is for any group. Ask if anyone has ever had the experience of trusting someone and having them violate that trust by breaking confidentiality. Ask them to talk about how they felt when it happened. Allow the group to talk about this as long as they need.

Have the group develop its own Rules and Consequences for how it will deal with any break in confidentiality. Be sure one of the rules describes what members of the group are to do if they know another member has broken confidentiality. Make sure there is consensus on the Rules and Consequences.

Give a copy of the "Confidentiality Contract" to every person in the group. Before the group members sign the contracts, have them write down the Rules and Consequences the group has adopted. After the contracts have been signed, collect them and keep them as long as the group continues to meet.

Activity 2
Past Histories

In any group, there are often people who have past histories with each other, meaning they have already had some contact or have formed some opinion of each other. However, in a group of people who go to the same school, *most* of the group members will have past histories! If the past histories are positive or neutral, there will be little or no interference in developing trust and acceptance within the group. However, if the past histories are negative, this will have a negative influence on how members of the group relate to each other. Frequently, these negative feelings lie just below the surface but are never discussed. Any deep bonding within the group is practically impossible with this kind of undercurrent.

After giving this explanation of past histories, tell the group members you will go around the circle, asking each person to talk about the past histories they share with the other members of the group.

If the past history is positive or neutral, have the group members give a short explanation of the relationship or situation.

If the past history is negative, have the group members talk about:
(1) what they will need to do, and
(2) what they will need from the other person in order to work through the negative memories.

Process:
How did you feel when you or others were discussing past histories, both positive and negative?

How hard is it for you to deal with negative feelings?

What would probably have happened if these negative feelings had never been discussed in our group?

Activity 3
Go-Arounds

Go-arounds are a wonderful way to warm-up a group and to insure that each group member participates at least once during the group session. The group leader or one of the group members can be in charge of choosing or inventing the go-around for a group session.

1. Tell how you are feeling on a scale from one to ten, with ten being terrific.

2. Share a personal "high" or "low" experience since the last group session.

3. Tell about a significant goal that directs your life.

4. Share an important thing you have discovered about yourself recently.

5. What was the last personal risk you took or new behavior you tried? What happened?

6. Observe three minutes of silence. Talk about what was going on inside you and what you observed happening in the group during that time.

7. Describe yourself as an animal, a flower or plant, and as a song. Tell why you made those choices.

8. If you inherited a million dollars today, what would you do with it? How much of what you would do with a million dollars could you do *without* a million dollars?

9. Talk about the last time someone wouldn't listen to you and what you did.

10. Who is the most important person in your life, and what kind of relationship do you have with this person?

11. What is the characteristic in people that you most admire?

12. Complete this sentence: I used to be... but now I'm....

13. If you knew you were going to die in 24 hours, how would you spend the time?

14. What is the worst thing that one person can do to another?

15. If you could go back and change one thing you have done, what would it be?

16. In what ways will you raise your children the same or differently from the way you have been raised?

17. If you could wake up tomorrow with a new ability or talent, what would it be?

18. Five years from now, how do you think you are going to feel about the things you do now? What might you wish you had changed?

19. When was the last time you cried? What had happened?

20. What is a risk for personal growth that you would like to take this week? (Open the next group session by going around the circle to see how each person did.)

Process:

What person did you learn the most about in this go-around?

What did you find yourself wanting the group to know about you, or what did you want to know about another group member?

Whom do you feel was especially open and honest during this go-around?

Activity 4
Stringing Along

The group leader holds a ball of string or yarn. As the group discussion begins, the ball of string is passed to the first person who speaks, with the group leader holding the end. The ball of string continues to be passed to each person who speaks, with the previous person continuing to hold onto their section of string.

At the end of the group discussion, the network that is formed by the string is examined by the group.

Process:

Who spoke most frequently? Who spoke least frequently?

What patterns of response do you see within the group?

What can the group do to help each member participate fully?

Activity 5
Tell Me Your Life Story
—You Have One Minute

The group selects one of its members to present a one-minute autobiography. The "autobiographer" may do anything to get others to listen. The group will do everything they can *not* to listen.

After the first "autobiographer" has finished, choose 1 or 2 other group members to do their autobiographies.

Allow the "autobiographers" to discuss their frustration at wanting to talk about something important to them and not having anyone listen. Discuss how we all do this unintentionally at times. Ask how other members of the group were feeling during this activity.

Then go around the circle, asking group members to talk about why they are here—what personal characteristics or feelings they want to change, what personal relationships they would like to improve, or what they hope to gain from the group experience.

Process:
What similarities in situations and feelings are there among members of the group?

Whose situation seems most like yours? Did you know that?

Whom do you feel you learned the most about today?

Activity 6
The Outsider

This activity allows group members to focus on how it feels to be left out of a group. Form small groups of 2 or 3 members and have each group decide who will be the "outsider."

When you give the signal, the "outsiders" are to try to find a way to break into or be accepted by their small group. The "outsiders" may use any method they choose, as long as it is non-violent. Before beginning, the other members of the small groups decide how they are going to respond to the "outsider."

Give the signal for the "outsiders" to begin. After 1 to 2 minutes, call time. Then another person from the small group is chosen to be the "outsider." Continue this until every person has experienced being the "outsider."

Process:
How did you feel when you were the "outsider?"

How did you feel when you were keeping out the "outsider?"

What methods for breaking in or being accepted seemed to work best?

Have you ever felt like this with "groups" in this school? What are the different "groups" in this school?

How do they keep "outsiders" out, and why do you think "groups" do this?

How do we unintentionally make others feel like "outsiders?"

What are the different "groups" within this group?

What would it take for the different "groups" to feel closer?

Activity 7
Labels are for Cans, Not for People

How we relate to people often changes because of the labels other people put on us or because of the labels we put on ourselves. To experience this, the group members are going to be "labeled," by having a label pinned or taped where they can't see it. Their label will instruct the other group members how to respond to them. After everyone has been "labeled," the group members are to walk around the room, making contact with everyone in the group. They are to talk about the following topic: a time when they made someone really angry but didn't mean to.

Two things will be happening simultaneously in each person's conversation. When Person A is speaking to Person B, Person B will respond by doing what Person A's label says. When Person B is speaking to Person A, Person A will respond by doing what Person B's label says.

Process:
How did your behavior change as you saw people responding to your label?

What does this say about labels we put on ourselves and other people?

What does this say about what we need from each other at all times and especially within this group?

How did you feel during this activity?

What are some examples of actual labels people put on each other?

Labels

Walk away while I am still talking.

Show that you think I am stupid.

Smile at me and welcome me.

Ask my opinion.

Show that you don't trust me.

Help me.

Ask me about my haircut or where I got my clothes.

Show that you don't understand me.

Just stare at me.

Show that you admire me.

Look at my left shoulder when I talk.

Laugh at me.

Put me down.

Yell at me whenever I use the word "I".

Show that you pity me.

Don't even notice I am here.

Show that you care about me.

Interrupt me every time I speak.

Talk to me but keep backing away.

Loudly tell the rest of the group what I tell you.

Activity 8

Between the Sexes

Have all the females make a small circle in the middle of the room. Then have the males make a circle around the females.

The inner circle—the females—talks about the following questions: What are some advantages males have in our society? What are some things that males seem to find especially hard to do? What are some possible explanations for this?

The outer circle—the males—sits quietly and listens. When everyone in the inner circle has had a chance to respond, everyone changes places, with the outer circle becoming the inner circle.

The new inner circle—the males—answers the same questions about males for themselves. Then they talk about the same questions for females: What are some advantages females have in our society? What are some things that females seem to find especially hard to do? What are some possible explanations for this?

The outer circle—the females—sits quietly and listens. When everyone in the inner circle has had a chance to respond, everyone changes places again, with the outer circle becoming the inner circle. The new inner circle—the females—answers the same questions about females for themselves.

Form one large circle to consider additional questions: What are some other things that males and females don't understand about each other? What do males look for in a date? What do females look for in a date? Is it okay for a female to ask out a male? If so, who pays? How should a female handle a male who is pressuring her to go further than she wants? Why are some things okay for males but not for females?

Process:
What did you learn about males or females that surprised you?

What needs to be talked about more?

Phase II
Moving Toward Understanding
and Acceptance

Activity 9
I See, I Know, I Believe

Group members form pairs, getting with a person they don't know as well as others.

The group members make a series of "I see..." statements about their partner. These statements must be limited to things a person can *see* about their partner. For example:
"I see you have blue eyes."
"I see you are smiling."
"I see you are looking away from me."

Next, the group members make a series of "I know..." statements. These statements must be limited to things the group members *know* are true about their partner. For example:
"I know you have only talked twice in this group."
"I know you live with your mother."
"I know you spend a lot of time with Karen."

Last, the group members make a series of "I believe..." statements. These statements must be based on what the group members *believe* is true about their partner. For example:
"I believe you are a happy person."
"I believe you are shy."
"I believe you enjoy this group."

Process:
How accurate were your statements to your partner?

Which kind of statement was hardest, or easiest, for you?

How did you feel while your partner was making statements to you?

Go-around the circle, having group members talk about the difference between what others "see, know, or believe" about them and what they "see, know, or believe" about themselves.

Activity 10
First Impressions

Ask group members to write down five "first impressions" they believe others generally have of them.

Then have group members write down one first impression they had about each person in the group.

When group members volunteer to hear the first impressions other members of the group had about them, the group members read what they had written for that person. Then the volunteers read their list of the five "first impressions" they believe others have of them.

Process:

How similar are the "first impressions" you believe others have of you and the ones they actually had?

If the first impressions of others are different, how do you explain this?

Are there any first impressions others had about you that you want to be different? What do you need to begin doing?

Activity 11
Extremes

This activity allows group members to compare their positions on several issues and to discuss their feelings about the issues. The group members will indicate their response to each question by physically positioning themselves on an imaginary line going from one corner of the room to the opposite corner. Each time a question is read, the leader indicates the location of each extreme.

For example, "How often do you talk to people you don't already know?"

The leader says, "If your answer is *always*, take this position (indicates one corner). If your answer is *never*, take this position (indicates the opposite corner). If your answer is somewhere in between, position yourself where you feel you belong."

When the group members have taken their positions, have them tell the people on both sides of them:
(1) their reasons for choosing that position, and
(2) how they feel about where they are.

Have the people at opposite ends of the imaginary line talk to each other across the room, discussing their responses to the same two questions.

Use this process for each question.

How far would you go to be accepted by others?
Extremes: *I would do anything—I would do nothing.*

How do you feel about marriage for yourself?
Extremes: *I plan to get married as soon as possible—I will never get married.*

What is most important to you in a romantic relationship?
Extremes: *Being best friends—Physical attraction*

What is the most important thing people can do with their lives?
Extremes: *Make money—Help others*

How close are you to your family?
Extremes: *We are best friends—We are complete strangers.*

How do you feel about yourself?
Extremes: *I accept everything about myself—I accept nothing about myself.*

Activity 12
My Mother, My Father, My Self

Ask the group members to describe themselves as:

(1) their mother sees them,
(2) their father sees them,
(3) they see themselves, and as
(4) they would like to become.

Process:

What do you need to do to be the person you want to become?

What do you need to do to be seen more accurately by your mother or father?

What do you realize about yourself for the first time by doing this?

Activity 13
Self-Portrait

Ask the group members to "draw a picture" of themselves using words. Have them choose five descriptive words from the list given or use any other words they wish.

Have them tell the group:
(1) Which descriptive words they chose
(2) What they do that makes those words accurate descriptions of them
(3) What they get out of acting in those ways

Then have group members choose three words that they *wish* described them. Have them talk about:
(1) What people do who are like that, and
(2) How being that way would help them.

Members may ask the entire group or a group member to pick the five words they feel best describe them. Have the group or group member give specific examples that show the accuracy of the descriptive words chosen.

Process:

How do you feel after doing this activity?

Whom do you see differently?

What did you learn about how you are perceived by others?

Some Descriptive Words

Forgiving	Boring	Moody
Selfish	Extroverted	Depressed
Stimulating	Indifferent	Trusting
Open	Giving	Funny
Angry	Follower	Leader
Assertive	Affectionate	Sympathetic
Shy	Aloof	Nervous
Thoughtful	Opinionated	Creative
Vengeful	Judgmental	Enthusiastic
Sensitive	Aggressive	Sentimental
Distracted	Confident	Competitive
Accepting	Attentive	Quiet
Serious	Forgetful	Honest
Loyal	Talkative	Thoughtless
Mellow	Generous	Dependable
Unthinking	Passive	Understanding

Activity 14
A Focus on Feelings

On a big pad of paper list the following feelings:

Anger
Fear
Happiness
Jealousy
Sadness
Guilt
Love
Shame
Hatred
Loneliness
Hope

Have the group members form pairs, getting with someone they have not worked with yet. Ask the group members to identify the feeling from the list they experience most frequently. Have them tell their partner about the most recent situation in which they felt this way.

Have the group members come back to the circle after they have finished their discussions. Then the group leader talks with the group about how our feelings are caused by our thoughts, giving several personal examples to illustrate the idea.

Have the group members talk to the group about the feeling they selected, again giving the most recent situation in which it was experienced. However, this time also ask group members to identify the thoughts they had to go with the feeling.

Process:
What did you learn about yourself or your partner by doing this activity?

What other feelings could you choose to experience in the situation you discussed?

In what other situations could you choose different feelings?

Phase III
Developing Mutual Support and Personal Growth

Activity 15

Self-Disclosure

The group leader introduces this activity with a statement like the following one:

"Most of us are afraid of looking bad in front of others, and this fear makes it hard to risk being genuine and open about who we are and how we feel. Ironically, though, it usually works in just the opposite way. When we are closed about who we are and how we feel, people will often misunderstand us. Misunderstanding frequently leads to trouble between people. When we are open about who we are and how we feel, other people generally end up accepting us more because they understand us better. We have helped them understand how to interpret the things we do."

"There is a tremendous relief that comes from being able to share a feeling we have kept stored inside. When we keep a feeling secret, from others or from ourselves, it actually controls us in a way it never can if we talk about it. Our fear of the feeling is what gives it power."

"Most of us choose one behavior we tend to use in situations where we feel afraid, embarrassed, ashamed, or inadequate in some way. Those behaviors are:

Silence:
If I don't say anything, no one will find out who I am.

Joking:
If I keep them laughing, no one will find out who I am.

Acting superior:
If I act like what we are doing is stupid, no one will find out who I am.

Acting confused:
If I act like I don't understand, no one will find out who I am."

Go around the circle, asking group members to identify the behavior they tend to use when they are uncomfortable in a situation. Ask them to talk about what it is they are afraid others will find out about them.

Process:

How do you feel?

Is there anything you would like to say in support of someone in the group?

Whom do you feel closer to as a result of this activity?

Activity 16
Proud Moments

The group leader makes an introductory statement similar to the following one:

"In our society, one of the hardest things for most people to do is to talk about one of their accomplishments. Most people are taught at an early age others don't like it when they brag. Unfortunately, many people don't realize bragging and quietly feeling good about something they have done are not the same thing."

"Self-esteem is how we feel about ourselves. How we feel about ourselves is determined by what we do. Learning to cherish and prize the things we do skillfully strengthens us and encourages us to do more. If all we can ever see are our weaknesses and our failures, our image of ourselves becomes as distorted as the image we see in a mirror at the carnival."

Go around the circle and ask group members to share one of their personally proud moments.

Process:
How hard was this for you to do? Why do you think that is?

What do you know and appreciate about another group member that you didn't know before?

Another time when you have achieved something important to you or are especially happy about something, will you share it with this group?

Activity 17
Secrets

Ask group members to write a secret about themselves on a piece of paper. This secret can be something they have thought or done but should be something they have never told anyone. Place the pieces of paper in a container and mix them up. The group members are to draw one of the secrets out of the container, making sure they do not get their own.

The group members read the secret they have drawn as if it were theirs, and they talk about how it feels. Afterwards, group members who have had a similar experience are asked to share and to talk about how they felt.

It is important for the group leader to emphasize that the purpose of this activity is to let people see that often others are better able to understand our experiences and feelings than we think. It is *critical* group members be at a stage of development in which they can respond in caring and empathic ways. It is also important to discuss with the group that people can only role play a situation from their own point of view. It is impossible to know another person's actual experiences, feelings, and responses. In doing this activity, people can only respond as *they* would feel.

Process:
How did you feel when you role played another person's secret?

How did you feel about the way group members responded to each other's secret?

What was this experience like for you?

Activity 18
Asking for Feedback

The group members choose a question from the list below, or they may ask their own question. They also choose the person they want to have answer the question. After the question is answered, other members of the group may also add their feedback, if invited to do so by the group member.

Before beginning, the group leader discusses the guidelines for giving and receiving feedback.

Stimulus Questions:
What do you think is my best quality?
What is something about me that you don't understand?
Describe how you see me as a person.
What kind of person do you think I get along with best?
Describe what you see as a weakness and a strength of mine.
In what ways do you think I work well with people?
What do you like best about me? Least?
What do you see me doing in ten years?
How well do you think I deal with anger?
Do you notice something that seems to be hard for me?
How accepting would you say I am?
What do I seem to enjoy doing most?
In what ways do you think I am assertive?
How have I changed since this group began?
What is something you have always wanted to tell me?

Process:
Which do you find harder, giving or receiving feedback?

How do you feel about the feedback you received?

Is there something else you would like to ask someone?

Activity 19

Dream Group

The group leader gives information to the group about dreams and also about techniques for remembering and interpreting dreams.

Then the group leader makes a statement similar to the following one:

"People are the experts when it comes to interpreting their own dreams. Sometimes, though, it is easier to interpret dreams in a group setting where the people know and appreciate each other. Just talking about dreams often helps people see a connection between what happens in their dreams and what happens in their lives. Also, other people will sometimes see a meaning or relationship in a dream that a person has overlooked. However, in helping others interpret their dreams, this is the rule we will follow: if the explanation feels right to the person, then it probably is. If it doesn't feel right, then it's not."

Have group members begin keeping a record of their dreams and invite them to bring in descriptions of the dreams that they would like to share or would like help in interpreting.

Process:

What would you guess is the general message of your dream?

What significant events happened within two or three days of the dream?

What area of your life or what relationship does your dream focus upon?

Is there a literal meaning to your dream?

What is the setting of your dream? What happens in places such as this?

Who are the people in your dream? What are they like? How do you feel about them? What is your relationship with them like?

Can you feel the part of you that is like these people?

What are the objects in your dream?

What is the major action in the dream? What does it remind you of in your life?

How do you feel in the dream? What do the feelings in your dream remind you of in your life?

Activity 20
In the Mind's Eye

Visualization is one of the most powerful tools available to people. Visualization is used by athletes to improve their performance, by cancer patients to fight their illnesses, and by businessmen to improve their sales production. It can be used to develop or improve a specific skill such as public speaking, shooting free throws, or learning to type. Visualization can be used for personal growth or to improve any aspect of life. It can be used to develop or improve personal characteristics such as becoming more outgoing, being more confident in social situations, being more assertive, or experiencing greater joy in life.

In using visualization, you picture yourself *already having accomplished your goal*. In this way, you will be picturing the positive outcome that you desire to experience. The more vividly you can picture this, the more effective it will be! It is very important to become completely involved in the visualization you create. "*See*" yourself accomplishing your goal, "*feel*" your reaction and sense the reactions of others, "*hear*" yourself and others speaking of your accomplishment, and enjoy the "*smell*" and "*taste*" of victory! By doing your visualization once a day for several weeks, you will begin to create the changes you desire.

Visualization is most effective when combined with relaxation techniques. When the mind and body are relaxed, they are more receptive to suggestion—both positive and negative! Be sure to always visualize positive outcomes and goals, seeing yourself already doing that which you want to accomplish or experience.

Visualization Exercise

Relaxation
The group leader has the group members get as comfortable as possible and then says *slowly*:

> Close your eyes. Begin to breathe deeply....
> Breathe in through your nose and hold the breath
> for as long as you comfortably can.... Then

breathe out slowly through slightly parted lips.... As you inhale, picture yourself breathing in peace, love, and joy.... As you exhale, picture yourself breathing out conflict, pain, and worry.... Feel a wave of serenity move through your body.... (Allow a few moments for this.)

And now I want you to use your imagination and feel your body relaxing as I ask you to do so.... And the relaxing power is now coming into the toes of both of your feet at the same time.... It's moving right on down into the arches, into the heels, and right on up to your ankles.... Completely relaxed, completely relaxed.... And the relaxing power is now moving on up your legs to the knees, relaxing all the muscles as it goes.... And on up your legs now to the thighs, and to the hips, just completely relaxing.... And your full attention is on the sound of my voice as the relaxing power moves into the fingers of both of your hands, just completely relaxing your hands.... And it's now moving up into your forearms, relaxing your forearms, and on up into your upper arms, just completely relaxing your upper arms.... And I want you to feel the relaxing power come into the base of your spine.... And now it begins to move slowly up your spine and into the back of your neck and shoulder muscles.... And the back of your neck and shoulder muscles are now loose and limp, loose and limp.... Just completely relaxed.... And the relaxing power now moves up the back of your neck and into your scalp, and your scalp is completely relaxed.... And the relaxing power is now draining down into your facial muscles, and your facial muscles are relaxed.... Your jaw is relaxed.... Allow a little space between your teeth.... And your throat is relaxed.... Your entire body is now relaxed all over in every way.... All tension is gone from your body and mind.... *

Visualization

The group leader continues to say *slowly*:

> And now, begin to create a special place in your mind's eye where you can go anytime to experience peace and tranquility.... This is your special place.... Your special corner of the universe.... Be aware of the colors and sights as you create your special place.... Smell the scents and aromas.... Feel the textures in your special place.... Enjoy all you see and feel and hear and smell in your special place.... Now look around and find a comfortable place to sit down.... And, if you like, draw someone you want to be with into your special place.... Have an enjoyable, loving conversation with this person.... Or, if you prefer, remain alone in your special place, content with your thoughts.... (Allow several minutes for this.)

> And now I want you to come back. On the count of three, you will be refreshed and alert, feeling strong and relaxed. Number One, feel the blood flowing through your arms and legs. Number Two, feel a sense of balance and harmony. And Number Three, open your eyes and feel good.

Process

What did you experience and how did you feel?

If you brought someone into your special place, whom did you invite?

If you remained alone, what feelings or new awareness did you experience?

* Relaxation technique used with permission of Dick Sutphen/Valley of the Sun, Malibu, CA.

Other Possible Visualizations

Visualizations can be developed for any situation. Simply use the format given, starting with the relaxation techniques and inserting the new visualization in its proper place.

Self as a Child Visualization

And now, see yourself walking down a path along a seashore or perhaps through a meadow or in a sunny forest.... And as you continue along this path, you see a small child coming toward you.... As you continue along your way, you now see that it is yourself as a small child coming toward you.... And you are smiling, and you greet each other with joy and with a hug.... You walk along the path together, talking with each other.... And you are telling your small child self all that you understand now that you didn't understand at that age.... (Allow several minutes for this.).... And your small child self reminds you of all that you hoped for and planned to do as you got older.... (Allow several minutes for this.).... And you thank each other for all you have shared and given to each other.... And you say good-bye for now....

And now I want you to come back. On the count of three, you will be refreshed and alert, feeling strong and relaxed. Number One, feel the blood flowing through your arms and legs. Number Two, feel a sense of balance and harmony. And Number Three, open your eyes and feel good.

Relationships Visualization

And now, I want you to picture your favorite place.... This is the place you would rather be than any other.... It is a serene and beautiful place.... In this place, you feel peaceful and balanced and strong.... Here, you feel a sense of harmony with yourself and the world as in no other place.... And now draw into your special place someone with whom you want to improve your relationship.... Greet this person and say thanks for coming.... Find a spot where both of you can be comfortable and secure.... Invite this person to talk with you about your relationship.... Begin by telling this person how you feel and what you need in the relationship.... Do this lovingly.... (Allow several minutes for this).... Now listen as the person tells you what he or she feels and needs in the relationship.... This is done lovingly.... (Allow several minutes for this).... Acknowledge each other for what you have shared and say goodbye for now....

And now I want you to come back. On the count of three, you will be refreshed and alert, feeling strong and relaxed. Number one, feel the blood flowing through your arms and legs. Number Two, feel a sense of balance and harmony. And Number Three, open your eyes and feel good.

Specific Skill or Personal Characteristic Visualization

And now, I want you to picture yourself already having acquired the skill or personal characteristic you would like to experience.... See every detail of what you do or experience.... See yourself performing perfectly or behaving in precisely the way you want.... Feel your reaction to your accomplishment.... Sense your feeling of confidence.... Enjoy your feeling of achievement.... See the reaction of others to your accomplishment.... See yourself repeating this performance anytime you desire to do so.... Do this now while I remain quiet for awhile.... (Allow several minutes for this).... From this moment on, this *is* your experience. You have the ability to experience any reality you desire.

And now I want you to come back. On the count of three, you will be refreshed and alert, feeling strong and relaxed. Number One, feel the blood flowing through your arms and legs. Number Two, feel a sense of balance and harmony. And Number Three, open your eyes and feel good.

Activity 21

Strokes

This activity is an excellent way to bring positive closure to a group before a major holiday or at the end of the year. It is also a good way to give group members positive strokes at any time of the year. Three different ways of doing this activity are described below:

1. The group leader gives the members enough pieces of paper so they have one for each person in the group. The group members write a message to each member of the group. The message is a statement of what is special about that person to the one writing. The messages are to be as specific as possible, focusing on an ability or characteristic of the person and giving examples of what the person does the writer enjoys or admires. The group members are encouraged to sign their messages. The messages are then folded, the name is written on the outside, and they are given to the group members.

2. The group leader tapes a blank sheet of paper on the back of each group member. Then everyone moves around the room, writing a special message on each group member's paper. When everyone has finished, the papers are removed and read.

3. The group leader asks a group member to act as record keeper. The group member on the record keeper's right becomes the "target" of a positive bombardment. Each of the group members, whenever they are ready, says a word out loud which describes something special about the "target." The record keeper makes a list of all the words given. When each group member has given a word, the list is passed around, and the group members sign their names next to the words they gave. The list is given to the "target."

Process

Each group member is invited to share the feedback that was the most meaningful, to ask for clarification on any messages or words, or to express the feelings experienced during this activity.

Unit V
Classroom Presentations

Chapter 19
Fourth Grade Substance Abuse Prevention Program

Session I

I. Introductions

Introduce yourselves and explain what you do as a peer counselor.

Tell the students that you will be with them for four sessions. Explain you will be talking about some things that are very important to you and you think will be important to them.

In this session you will be talking about how important it is to feel good about yourself as a person.

In the second session you will be talking about feelings and about how important it is to be able to tell our feelings to someone.

In the third session you will be talking about being a better listener and learning to communicate better with others.

In the fourth session you will be talking about substance abuse. People sometimes use alcohol or other drugs as a way to feel better when they don't feel good about themselves, when they don't talk about their feelings, and when it is hard for them to communicate what they need.

II. Warm Fuzzies
Tell the students that you will start this session by reading them a story, called *Warm Fuzzies (and Cold Pricklies)*.

After you have finished the story, have the students brainstorm examples of warm fuzzies and cold pricklies to make sure they understand the concept. They may have trouble with this at first, and need you to help them get started. (Describe briefly the rules for brainstorming: (1) All ideas are good; (2) The purpose is to come up with as many ideas as possible; and (3) A time limit is set.)

III. Process
Which do you think are more common, warm fuzzies or cold pricklies? Why do you think this is?

Which is harder, giving or receiving a warm fuzzy?

What happens to people when they get a warm fuzzy? What about a cold prickly?

What might happen to people who get mostly cold pricklies all their lives?

Is it okay to give yourself a warm fuzzy?

Does anyone have a story about a time you gave a warm fuzzy (or cold prickly) to someone?

IV. Challenge
Ask the students to keep track of how many warm fuzzies and how many cold pricklies they give this week. Ask them to notice how they feel about themselves when they give warm fuzzies and when they give cold pricklies.

V. Question Box
Leave a question box in the room for students who would like to ask questions but don't feel comfortable asking them in front of the class. Tell them you will go through the questions each week and will answer as many as you can during the session.

Thank the teacher and the students for having you as a guest in their classroom. Make sure they know when you will return.

Warm Fuzzies (and Cold Pricklies)

Long ago only little people lived on the Earth. They lived in the village of Swabeedoo, and so they called themselves Swabeedoo-dahs. They were very happy little people, and they went around with big smiles and cheerful greetings.

What the Swabeedoo-dahs enjoyed most was giving warm fuzzies to each other. Each of them carried a shoulder bag, and these bags were always filled with warm fuzzies. Whenever two Swabeedoo-dahs would meet, they would give each other a warm fuzzy. It was a way of saying, "Hello. I like you." It felt *really good* to get so many warm fuzzies. It made each of the Swabeedoo-dahs feel noticed and appreciated, and then they wanted to give more warm fuzzies in return. This made their lives together very happy indeed.

Outside the village, in a cold, dark cave, lived a great green troll. He didn't really like to live all by himself, and sometimes he was lonely. But he couldn't seem to get along with anyone, and he definitely didn't like exchanging warm fuzzies. "It's just not cool," he said.

One evening the troll walked into town and was greeted by a kindly little Swabeedoo-dah. "Hasn't this been a fine Swabeedoo-dah day?" said the little person with a smile. "Here, have a warm fuzzy. This one is special. I saved it just for you."

The troll looked around to make sure no one else was listening. Then he whispered in the little Swabeedoo-dah's ear, "Haven't you heard that if you give away too many warm fuzzies, one of these days you're gonna run out?"

He saw the look of surprise and fear on the little Swabeedoo-dah's face. Then he added, "Right now, I'd say you've got about seventy-three warm fuzzies in your fuzzy-bag there. Better go easy on givin' em' away!" With that, the troll padded away on his big green feet, leaving a very worried and confused Swabeedoo-dah standing there.

Now the troll knew that there was an unending supply of warm fuzzies. He knew that as soon as you give a warm fuzzy to someone another one comes to take its place, and you can never, ever run out of warm fuzzies in your whole life. But he counted on the trusting nature of the little Swabeedoo-dahs. So he told his fib and went back to his cave and waited.

Well, he didn't have to wait long. The first person to come along and greet the little Swabeedoo-dah was an old friend of his. This friend was surprised to find that when he gave a warm fuzzy, he received only a strange look in return and was told to beware of running out of warm fuzzies. That same afternoon, the friend told seven other Swabeedoo-dah's who told nineteen other Swabeedoo-dah's, "Sorry, no warm fuzzy this time. I'm a little low."

By the next day, word had spread over the entire village. Everyone had suddenly begun to save their warm fuzzies. They still gave some away, but only occasionally. *"Very carefully,"* they said.

The little Swabeedoo-dahs even began to be suspicious of each other and to hide their bags of warm fuzzies under their pillows at night. People began to trade warm fuzzies for things, instead of giving them away. There were even reports of robberies of warm fuzzies. Some nights it wasn't even safe to be out and about.

At first the troll was pleased. Now when he went into town, he was no longer greeted with smiles or offered warm fuzzies. Instead, the little people looked at him the way they looked at each other, suspiciously. He rather liked that. To him that was just facing reality. "It's the way the world is," he said.

But things kept getting worse. More and more Swabeedoo-dahs came down with a disease known as "hardening of the heart," and a few of the little people died. Now all of the happiness was gone from the village of Swabeedoo.

When the troll heard what was happening, he said to himself, "Gosh! I just wanted 'em to see how the world is. I didn't mean for 'em to die!" He kept wondering what he should do. Then he thought of a plan!

Deep in his cave, the troll had discovered a secret mine of cold pricklies. He had spent many years digging the cold pricklies out of the mountain because he liked their cold and prickly feel. He decided to share them with the Swabeedoo-dahs. He filled hundreds of bags with cold pricklies and took them into the village.

When the people saw the bags of cold pricklies, they were relieved and took them gratefully. At least now they had something to give each other! The only trouble was it was just not as much fun to give a cold prickly. *Getting a cold prickly* gave you a funny feeling, too. It was nice to get something from other people, but it was hard to know for sure what they meant. After all, cold pricklies *are* cold and prickly.

Some of the Swabeedoo-dahs went back to giving warm fuzzies. Each time a warm fuzzy was exchanged, it made both of the little people feel very happy. Perhaps that was partly because it was so unusual to get a warm fuzzy, with so many cold pricklies being exchanged.

But giving warm fuzzies never really came back into style in Swabeedoo. A few of the little people found that they could keep giving warm fuzzies away without ever running out. The art of giving warm fuzzies had been lost in Swabeedoo.

Now suspicion was in the minds of most of the little people. You could hear it in their reaction. "A warm fuzzy?! I wonder what he wants from me?"

Author Unknown
Condensed and Revised
Based on *The Original Warm Fuzzy Tale*, by Claude Steiner

Session II

I. Challenge Report.

Ask the students what they discovered in doing their challenge.

Review your discussion about warm fuzzies and cold pricklies and how they make people feel. Explain that you are going to talk more about feelings during this session.

II. "Feelings" Demonstration.

Ask for five volunteers. Give each volunteer a piece of paper with one of the following directions: Show A Tired Walk, Show An Angry Walk, Show A Happy Walk, Show A Frightened Walk, and Show A Sad Walk.

After each demonstration, ask the class to guess what feeling was being shown. After all five demonstrations have been given, ask the students how they were able to guess feelings when no words were used. Explain we all communicate even when we don't use words. Remind them of the times when the class guessed the wrong feeling. Explain that if we want to be sure people understand how we feel, we have to tell them. Otherwise they may misunderstand us.

III. "Show Me the Story."

Ask for five volunteers to do another demonstration. Tell the volunteers you are going to read a short story to them. Each time you pause, you want one of the volunteers to show how he or she would be feeling if that was actually happening. The first time you pause, you want the first volunteer to show the feeling, and so on.

"Let me tell you a story about my terrible day at school.... The first thing that happened was that everyone laughed at me because of my haircut.... I was so upset, I didn't hear the bell ring.... When I came running in late, everyone laughed at me again.... When my teacher said I had to stay in at recess, I was so mad!... All morning, everything I did turned out all wrong.... But during recess my teacher talked to me, and then I felt so much better.... I still don't like my haircut, but I know it will grow out.... Some of my friends told me they *like my haircut*.... And some of them told me they *like me*, so what difference does a haircut make?

IV. Identify Feelings.
Ask the class to brainstorm a list of feelings, including the feelings they saw during the demonstrations. (The list will include feelings such as angry, sad, happy, afraid, confused, depressed, worried, sorry, lonely, hurt, and so on.) Write this list on a section of the board where it can remain while you do the next part of the presentation.

V. Recognize Feelings.
Explain to the students it is very important to learn to *recognize* what we are feeling. Tell them our bodies always give us signals to understand how we feel.

Ask the students to brainstorm different ways our bodies can signal us about our feelings. (The list will include things such as: stomach ache, headache, clenched teeth, clenched fists, stiff neck, red face, tense muscles, crying, heart pounding, and so on.)

Explain to the students not everyone reacts the same way to a feeling. Some people get a headache when they are angry, and others get a stomach ache. Ask the students to pair some of the feelings they identified with some of the body reactions they listed. Emphasize although other people might have a certain reaction to a feeling, it is learning to recognize *your* reaction that counts.

VI. Express Feelings.
Explain to the students there are no "good" or "bad" feelings. Feelings just are. It is what we *do* about our feelings that can be good or bad. Ask the students to brainstorm positive ways to handle feelings. (The list will include things such as: talk to someone, exercise, write down how you feel in a letter or journal, go for a walk, play with the dog/cat, remember that the bad times pass, and so on.)

Draw a circle around "talk to someone" on the list and have the students identify all the different people they could talk to if they wanted.

VII. Process.

Why do you think it is important to let people know how you feel?

Why do you think people laugh sometimes when someone shows their feelings, especially when someone cries?

What do you think people will do if others laugh when they show their feelings?

VIII. Challenge.

Ask the students to keep track of how often they talk about their feelings and how often they cover them up this week.

IX. Question Box.

Answer as many questions as time permits.

Session III

I. Challenge Report.

Ask the students what they discovered in doing their challenge.

Point out that sometimes it is hard for people to talk about their feelings because other people don't listen. Also, sometimes it is hard to know what to say. Tell the students that you are going to be practicing both parts of communication in this session.

II. "Listening" Demonstration

1st peer counselor:
Let me tell you about my weekend. It was so much fun! I....

2nd peer counselor:
I had a great weekend, too!

1st peer counselor:
Yes, well, that's good. We went to San Diego, and the weather was beautiful. We....

2nd peer counselor:
When the weather is nice, I like to play tennis.

1st peer counselor:
Oh, good. I wanted to tell you about San Diego....

2nd peer counselor:
I remember the last time I was in San Diego. I played in a tennis tournament.

1st peer counselor:
Uhh, that's nice.... We got to go down to the harbor, and we saw some boats....

2nd peer counselor:
Boating is my next favorite thing to do after tennis.

1st peer counselor:
Oh? Well, anyway, after that we rode down this winding road right by the ocean....

2nd peer counselor:
My grandmother lives on a winding road by the ocean.

1st peer counselor: *Yeah, well, that's nice.... Listen, I'll talk to you later.*

III. Process.
Although this was exaggerated, has anything like this ever happened to you?

How did you feel?

How many of you have ever done this?

Why do you think this happens?

Do you think people don't talk about how they feel sometimes because no one listens? If people are trying to say something that is hard to talk about, how long do you think they will keep trying?

IV. Communication Activity.
There are two main parts to communication. One involves being a good listener so that you know how the other person feels. The other one involves being willing to talk about how you feel and what you need.

People sometimes communicate things they don't really mean or don't help the situation. Tell the students you are going to have them do some role plays to demonstrate this point. Ask for 3-5 volunteers for each of the following situations:

Situation 1: John is a new student who is sitting alone in the cafeteria. Two of his classmates want to make friends, so they sit down at the table with him. But whenever they ask John a question, he just mumbles an answer. He turns his head away and pretends not to notice them. Finally they get up and walk away.

Process

What is the message the two students got from John?

What might John be feeling besides what it seems?

What could John say that would help them understand how he feels?

Situation 2: A group of classmates teases Anna because she always gets the best grades in the class. Whenever they tease her, Anna teases them back about always getting in trouble because they never do their work.

Process

How does Anna probably feel?

How do the people teasing Anna probably feel?

What could Anna say that would help them understand her better? What could they say that would help Anna understand them better?

What could they do to help each other?

Situation 3: Whenever teams are picked at recess, James is always the last person chosen. He acts like it doesn't bother him, but of course it does. The team captain who gets James says, "Why do we have to have James again?" James says, "That's okay. I don't really want to play anyway."

Process

How do you think James feels?

Which do you think is more important, winning or making sure everyone feels important?

What could be done so this doesn't happen to anyone?

What could James say to help them understand how he feels?

V. Challenge.
Ask the students to be a good listener for at least three different people this week. Ask them to talk to someone this week if there is something that has been bothering them.

VI. Question Box.
Answer as many questions as time permits.

Session IV

I. Challenge Report.
Ask the students what they discovered in doing their challenge.

II. Substance Abuse Discussion.
Make a statement to the students like the following one:

"When people haven't had many warm fuzzies all their lives, when it is hard for them to talk about their feelings, or when no one listens, people sometimes start drinking or doing other drugs to try to feel better. The problem is this doesn't change anything. The feelings are still there the next day. Sometimes, people become addicted, which means they can't stop drinking or doing the drug. Now they have another big problem on top of the other ones.

"Sometimes people start drinking or doing other drugs because they are bored or trying to be cool. Also, people sometimes start because their friends are doing it or because their friends talk them into it. We call this peer pressure. Yet what kind of friend would talk people into doing something that could hurt them?"

Tell the students that you would like them to make an agreement among their friends that *they* are not going to start and that they don't want *their friends* to start either. They can decide that it is *not cool* and that they don't need it.

Explain to the students that the certificate they are going to receive for participating in this program includes a contract for them to sign. Instruct the students to wait until everyone has received their certificate before signing theirs. Then individually have the students walk to the front of the room to receive their certificates. When the students all have their certificates, read the agreement on the certificate out loud. Ask if there are any questions. Then ask the students to sign their certificate *if* they are willing to make the agreement!

Go around to the students who have signed the agreement and sign it as their witness. Give the certificates to the teacher to sign and to return to the students. Ask the students to take their certificate home and to keep it where they will see it every day.

III. Process.
If one of your friends starts getting involved with alcohol or other drugs, what could you do to help? What about the person who doesn't have any friends?

IV. Question Box.
Answer as many questions as time permits.

V. Closure.
Say to the students: Since this is our last session, we'd like to do an activity called "I Learned...." (Write the words *I Learned....* on the board.) We'd like you to tell us what you have learned during the four sessions. Write their responses on the board and add one of yours.

Thank them for being so special and such a good audience.

Chapter 20

Sixth Grade Transition to the Junior High Program

Part I:
Introductions and Discussion
of the Differences at the Junior High

Introduce yourselves and explain what you do as a peer counselor. Explain that you've come to help prepare them for being at the junior high next year.

Involve the students in a discussion about the differences they will experience at the junior high. Include topics such as: using a locker, having a different teacher each hour, and being at a bigger school. Offer positive suggestions for dealing with these changes or other concerns that are raised by the students.

Tell the students that because a lot of people worry about being able to open their lockers, you are going to demonstrate how to use a combination lock. If possible, make arrangements to leave the lock with the class so they can practice. If this is not possible, pass the lock around the room so each person has a chance to try opening it.

Use the junior high handbook to discuss all the clubs and extracurricular activities that will be available to the students. Share some of your own experiences and activities and talk with the students about how much more fun school is when a person is involved.

Part II:
The Story of Kelly

Ask for five volunteers. Tell them they will need to remember a story. One volunteer stays in the class while the other four leave the room. One peer counselor reads the "Story Of Kelly" to the first volunteer in front of the class. The second volunteer is then brought into the room. The first volunteer tells the story to the second volunteer, who tells it to the third volunteer, etc. The fifth volunteer repeats the story to the class. Then the peer counselor rereads the "Story Of Kelly" so that the class can compare the versions.

Process

Identify all changes that were made in the story.

What does this say about stories that are repeated several times before they get to you?

Ask if anyone in the class has ever had a rumor going around the school about them. Ask a few of these students to talk about how they felt.

Explain the connection between rumors and physical fights in junior high. Ask the students what they already do or what they could start doing to stop rumors. Talk about the positive ways these situations are handled at the high school.

- Story of Kelly

Kelly is a ninth grader at Metropolis Junior High School in Flagstaff, Arizona. She moved to Arizona from Malibu, California in seventh grade.

Kelly is a friendly person who gets along with everyone. However, this Monday morning she is getting really angry at the people who keep coming to tell her about her boyfriend, Marc, and her best friend, Angie. Everybody says they were getting along *real good* at the party Friday night. So far, eleven "good" friends have told Kelly all about what happened. Kelly is so hurt, but she doesn't want anyone to know it.

Kelly was already upset about not getting to go to the party, but her parents said she had to stay home and babysit her brother, Jeffrey, and her sister, Lisa. Angie knew how disappointed Kelly was about not getting to go to the party.

Frank and Susan Roberts, Kelly's parents, have never liked Marc, but Angie has liked Marc since she was in seventh grade. Kelly doesn't know Angie likes Marc. The only time Kelly and Angie ever had a really big fight was right after Kelly moved to the junior high. There was a bad rumor going around about Kelly, and people always said that Angie was the one who started it. That was a long time ago, though, and until now Kelly and Angie have been best friends.

Part III:
Refusal Skills

Teach the refusal skills to the entire class, doing two or three different role plays to demonstrate them.

Then divide the class into smaller groups, one peer counselor to a group, so that the students can practice using the refusal skills. Use the role play topics as situations. One student will be the "target" of the peer pressure, and the others will put on the pressure as heavily as possible. After each role play has been processed, another student becomes the new "target."

Process

Ask the "targets" how they felt while resisting the pressure.

Help the students identify and analyze what happened during each role play situation, focusing in particular on what worked and what didn't work.

Ask the students to apply what they have seen during the role plays to their own lives. What are some of their own situations in which these refusal skills would be helpful? Practice using the refusal skills with their own situations.

Refusal Skills

Ways To Say "NO":

1. **Recruit a friend.** Find someone who feels the same way you do.

2. **Be a "broken record."** Use the same phrase over and over. "No thanks, I don't think I will," "No thanks, I don't think I will," and so forth.

3. **Delay.** Stall in making a decision. "I'll have to see if I can."

4. **Avoid the situation.** Don't go to the party to begin with or leave if things happen that you don't like.

5. **Personal credit.** Use your value as a person. "Do I have to do that to be your friend?"

6. **"Chicken" counter attack.** Turn it around. "*I'm* not the chicken. I know where *I* stand."

7. **Suggest an alternative.** When it is a friend you want to keep, suggest doing something different. "No, I don't really want to go to that party. Why don't we get a bunch of people together and go ice skating instead?"

8. **Just say no.** Say it any way you want or give any reason you want.

Role-Play Topics

You really don't like school. But you've decided that maybe if you were in school more, you'd do better. Then a buddy says, "Come on! We can find something better to do than stay in this dump!" What do you do?

You are at a concert. The three people next to you are smoking pot. Suddenly one of them asks you if you want some pot. You say no. Then they start laughing at you and calling you a "chicken." What do you do?

There is this really cool girl in your class who hangs around with all the really cool kids. You've wanted her to notice you for a long time. One day you run into her at the shopping mall, and she asks you if you want to hang out for a while. Later she says, "This is boring!! Let's go out back and have a cigarette." What do you do?

You and a friend have just gotten out of a movie when one of your neighbors, a high school junior, asks if you want a ride home. You can tell he has been drinking, and he is acting weird. You're kind of nervous, but you don't want to make a big deal out of it. What do you do?

You are at your best friend's house, and no one else is home. Your friend, Mike, knows where they keep the booze. He says no one will ever know. He does it all the time. Mike is pouring you a drink, but you really don't want it. What do you do?

You're down at the school playing basketball one Saturday morning with your best friend. Suddenly Bill pulls a can of spray paint out of his backpack and says, "Let's get even with that jerk, Mr. Smith! We'll write stuff about him on the walls. Come on!" What do you do?

You and a friend have gone to a school dance. Her mom was supposed to pick you up, but her older brother is there instead. He asks if you want to go to a party. You tell him that you have to be home by 10:30. He says, "Come on, we'll just tell them we had car trouble." What do you do?

Part IV:
Closure

Have the students take their seats again.

Ask them to tell you what is the most important thing they learned today.

Let the students know that peer counselors have support groups at the junior high. Explain these are small groups of students who get together once a week so they can talk about things that are going on in their lives. Tell them if they are interested in being in a support group to talk to their counselor at the junior high next year.

Thank them for their attention and for being such a good group!

References

Bach, R. (1977) *Illusions*. New York, NY: Dell Publishing.

Berger, S. (1983). *Divorce without victims: Helping children through divorce with a minimum of pain and trauma*. Boston, MA: Houghton Mifflin.

Bro, H.H. (1968). *Edgar Cayce on dreams*. New York, NY: Warner Books.

Canning, J. (1985). *Play times: A structured developmental play program utilizing trained peer facilitators*. Minneapolis, MN: Educational Media Corporation.

Delaney, G. (1979) *Living your dreams*. San Francisco, CA: Harper & Row, Publishers.

Domhoff, G.W. (1985). *The mystique of dreams: A search for utopia through Senoi dream theory*. Berkeley, CA: University of California Press.

Einstein, E. and Albert, L. (1986) *Strengthening your stepfamily*. Circle Pines, MN: American Guidance Service.

Faraday, A. (1974). *The dream game*. New York, NY: Harper & Row, Publishers.

Foster, E.S. (1989) *Energizers and icebreakers*. Minneapolis, MN: Educational Media Corporation.

Foster-Harrison, E.S. (1994). *More energizers and icebreakers*. Minneapolis, MN: Educational Media Corporation.

Hafen, B.Q. and Frandsen, K.J. (1986). *Youth suicide: Depression and loneliness*. Evergreen, CO: Cordillera Press.

Hazouri, S.P. and McLaughlin, M.S. (1993). *Warm ups & wind downs: 101 activities for moving and motivating groups*. Minneapolis, MN: Educational Media Corporation.

Ivey, A. and Hinkle, J. (1970). *The transactional classroom*. Unpublished paper, University of Massachusetts, Amherst, MA.

Kübler-Ross, E. (1975). *Death: The final stage of growth*. Englewood Cliffs, NJ: Prentice Hall.

Kübler-Ross, E. (1969). *On death and dying*. New York, NY: Macmillan Publishing.

Miller, M. (1989). *Suicide: The preventable death*. San Diego, CA: The Information Center.

Myrick, R.D. and Bowman, R.P. (1981). *Becoming a friendly helper: A handbook for student facilitators*. Minneapolis, MN: Educational Media Corporation.

Myrick, R.D. and Bowman, R.P. (1981, 1991). *Children helping children: Teaching students to become friendly helpers.* Minneapolis, MN: Educational Media Corporation.

Myrick, R.D. and Erney, T. (1978, 1984). *Caring and sharing: Becoming a peer facilitator.* Minneapolis, MN: Educational Media Corporation.

Myrick, R.D. and Erney, T. (1979, 1985). *Youth helping youth: A handbook for training peer facilitators.* Minneapolis, MN: Educational Media Corporation.

Myrick, R.D. and Folk, B.E. (1991). *Peervention: Training peer facilitators for prevention eduation.* Minneapolis, MN: Educational Media Corporation.

Myrick, R.D. and Folk, B.E. (1991). *The power of peervention: A manual for the trainers of peer facilitators.* Minneapolis, MN: Educational Media Corporation.

Myrick, R.D. and Sorenson, D.L. (1997). *Peer helping: A practical guide, second edition.* Minneapolis, MN: Educational Media Corporation.

Sorenson, D.L. (1992). *Conflict resolution and mediation for peer helpers.* Minneapolis, MN: Educational Media Corporation.

Sorenson, D.L. (1994). *Conflict management training activities.* Minneapolis, MN: Educational Media Corporation.

Steiner, C. (1977). *The Original warm fuzzy tale.* Rolling Hills Estate, CA: Jalmar Press.

Sturkie, J. and Gibson, V. (1998). *The peer helper's pocketbook.* San Jose, CA: Resource Publications.

Tindall, J.A. (1989) *Peer power, book 2, applying peer helper skills.* Bristol, PA: Accelerated Development.

Tindall, J.A. (1994) *Peer power, book 1 strategies for the professional leader.* Bristol, PA: Accelerated Development.

Tindall, J.A. (1994) *Peer power, book 1 workbook: Becoming an effective peer helper and conflict mediator, third edition.* Bristol, PA: Accelerated Development.

Tindall, J.A. (1994) *Peer power, book 2 strategies for the professional leader.* Bristol, PA: Accelerated Development.

Tindall, J.A. (1995) Peer programs: *An in-depth look at peer helping.* Bristol, PA: Accelerated Development.

Wegscheider, S. (1981). *Another chance: Hope and health for the alcoholic family.* Palo Alto, CA: Science and Behavior Books.